CRITICAL PERSPECTIVES ON LABOR UNIONS

ANALYZING THE ISSUES

CRITICAL PERSPECTIVES ON LABOR UNIONS

Edited by Rita Santos

Enslow Publishing

101 W. 23rd Street
Suite 240
New York, NY 10011
USA

enslow.com

Published in 2020 by Enslow Publishing, LLC
101 W. 23rd Street, Suite 240, New York, NY 10011

Library of Congress Cataloging-in-Publication Data

Names: Santos, Rita, editor.
Title: Critical perspectives on labor unions / edited by Rita Santos.
Description: New York : Enslow Publishing, 2020 | Series: Analyzing the issues | Audience: Grade 7-12. | Includes bibliographical references and index.
Identifiers: LCCN 2018024474| ISBN 9781978503304 (library bound) | ISBN 9781978505025 (pbk.)
Subjects: LCSH: Labor unions—United States—History—Juvenile literature.
Classification: LCC HD6508.25 .C75 2019 | DDC 331.880973—dc23
LC record available at https://lccn.loc.gov/2018024474

Printed in the United States of America

To Our Readers: We have done our best to make sure all website addresses in this book were active and appropriate when we went to press. However, the author and the publisher have no control over and assume no liability for the material available on those websites or on any websites they may link to. Any comments or suggestions can be sent by email to customerservice@enslow.com.

Photo Credits: Cover Tom Williams/CQ-Roll Call Group/Getty Images; cover and interior pages graphics Thaiview/Shutterstock.com (cover top, pp. 3, 6–7), gbreezy/Shutterstock.com (magnifying glass), Ghornstern/Shutterstock.com (chapter openers).

CONTENTS

INTRODUCTION

On March 25, 1911, a fire broke out on the eighth floor of the Triangle Shirtwaist Factory. The factory was rarely cleaned and full of highly flammable scraps of fabric, which helped the fire spread quickly. As the nearly five hundred workers attempted to escape the blaze they found the doors of the factory were locked from the outside. The factory owners kept the doors locked to cut down on the number of breaks workers could take. Many workers escaped by going up to the roof or cramming into the elevator. However, it took three minutes for the fire to overtake the only usable staircase.

When firefighters arrived hundreds of workers were still trapped on the eighth and ninth floors but the fire department's ladders only reached as high as the sixth floor. Workers crowded on to the building's only fire escape, but its poor construction caused it to collapse, killing twenty. The nets the firemen used to try to save the falling women weren't strong enough to catch them. Onlookers watched in horror as women began to jump from the building rather than burn to death. Sixty-two people leapt from the building. Of the 146 workers killed in the incident 123 were women, most of them young immigrants. The youngest known victims,

Kate Leone and Rosaria "Sara" Maltese, were only fourteen years old. This was the deadliest industrial disaster in New York's history.

The tragedy highlighted the issues the Women's Trade Union League (WTUL) had been fighting business owners about, and it galvanized workers. In a subsequent Women's Trade Union League meeting, activist Rose Schneiderman said, "I can't talk fellowship to you who are gathered here. Too much blood has been spilled. I know from my experience it is up to the working people to save themselves. The only way they can save themselves is by a strong working-class movement."[1]

The working-class movement Schneiderman was referring to was the growth of labor unions. A union is an organization of workers—most often tied to a particular job or trade—that is formed to protect and further the rights of workers. They are democratic organizations in which all members vote for leaders and to establish goals. In the aftermath of the Triangle Shirtwaist Factory tragedy, union ranks swelled. Due largely to union demands, numerous laws were enacted to prevent future tragedies.

The history of labor unions in the United States is stained with the blood of workers fighting for their rights. Before the rise of unions, conditions like those seen in the Triangle Shirtwaist Factory were common. Employers saw workers as expendable and had no compelling reasons to protect them or pay living wages. Labor was seen as easily replaceable so if one worker refused to suffer dangerous hazardous conditions for little pay, there was always someone waiting to take their place. Organizers realized the only way to solve the problem was to work together.

Organizers used a tactic known as "collective bargaining," where workers choose leaders to negotiate on behalf of all workers. Unions have used collective bargaining to argue for higher wages and shorter workdays for all workers and for child labor laws. But what really gives unions their power is the ability to strike. When businesses refuse to bend to the demands of workers the workers can retaliate by refusing to work. This is known as a strike. Business owners have a vested interest in avoiding strikes because of the loss of productivity and profits. A strike reminds business owners that without its employees the company could not run.

The 1935 Wagner Act officially protected the rights of citizens to unionize and go on strike. As unions became more powerful, workers saw their wages raise and their working conditions become safer. While unions remain popular with American citizens, more recent laws have diminished their power in many states. Some politicians believe that the need for unions has passed. They believe that compelling workers to join unions is discriminatory toward those who don't want to join.

In this volume, you will hear what people from different critical perspectives have to say on the topic of labor unions. It is a topic every citizen should put some thought into. As you read think about the effects unions have had on your life—or on your family's. Think about how unions function and whether or not more regulations should be put in place to protect them. Unions have been a major force of change throughout past generations and will most likely continue to be a force to be reckoned with in the future.

CHAPTER 1

WHAT ACADEMICS, EXPERTS, AND RESEARCHERS SAY

Unions have had a profound effect on American history. This affect is studied by historians, social scientists, and economists, among others. Academics remind us of what life was like for workers before the advent of labor unions. By studying and comparing the history of labor unions in the United States to that of other countries, researchers can gain a better understanding of the true power of the labor movement. This kind of comparison has helped researchers prove that a decline in labor unions is tied to a decline in wages for most workers. Along with reminding us why unions are beneficial to society, academics can also help us discover ways to strengthen existing unions. Using these insights, readers can form more informed opinions about the role of unions today.

"THE RISE AND FALL OF US LABOR UNIONS, AND WHY THEY STILL MATTER," BY JAKE ROSENFELD, FROM *THE CONVERSATION*, MARCH 27, 2015

The US labor movement was once the core institution fighting for average workers. Over the last half century, its ranks have been decimated. The share of the private sector workforce that is organized has fallen from 35% to approximately 6.5% today.

An expanding body of research demonstrates just what this loss has meant: the growth of economic and political inequality, stalled progress on racial integration and the removal of an established pathway for immigrant populations to assimilate economically.

Yet despite their decline, unions in the US retain some power in certain pockets of the country. Recent successes by these organizations reveal the importance of a revitalized labor movement for the nation's economic and civic health.

WHAT WENT WRONG?

By the mid-1950s, unions in the US had successfully organized approximately one out of every three non-farm workers. This period represented the peak of labor's power, as the ranks of unionized workers shrank in subsequent decades.

The decline gained speed in the 1980s and 1990s, spurred by a combination of economic and political developments. The opening up of overseas markets increased competition in many highly organized industries. Outsourcing emerged as a popular practice among employers seeking to compete in a radically changed environment. The deregulation of industries not threatened by overseas competition, such as trucking, also placed organized labor at a disadvantage as new nonunion firms gained market edge through lower labor costs.

Simultaneously, US employers developed a set of legal, semi-legal and illegal practices that proved effective at ridding establishments of existing unions and preventing nonunion workers from organizing. Common practices included threatening union sympathizers with dismissal, holding mandatory meetings with workers warning of the dire consequences (real or imagined) of a unionization campaign and hiring permanent replacements for striking workers during labor disputes.

A sharp political turn against labor aided these employer efforts. President Reagan's public firing of striking air traffic controllers vividly demonstrated to a weakened labor movement that times had changed. Anti-union politicians repeatedly blocked all union-backed efforts to re-balance the playing field, most recently in 2008-2009, with the successful Senate filibuster of the Employee Free Choice Act. EFCA would have made private sector organization efforts somewhat easier. The last major piece of federal legislation aiding unions in their organization efforts passed in 1935.

WHY DOES IT MATTER?

At its peak, the US labor movement stood alongside powerful business leaders and policymakers as key institutions shaping the nation's economy and polity. Union workers enjoyed healthy union "wage premiums," or increases in pay resulting directly from working under a union-negotiated contract.

But nonunion workers also benefited from a strong labor presence.

In research by Harvard University's Bruce Western and myself, we compared nonunion workers in highly organized locales and industries to nonunion workers in segments of the labor market with little union presence. After adjusting for core determinants of wages, such as education levels, we found that nonunion workers in strongly unionized industries and areas enjoyed substantially higher pay. Thus the economic benefits of a powerful labor movement redounded to unorganized workers as well as union members.

Early 20th-century unions—especially craft unions—engaged in a range of sometimes violent discriminatory practices. As a result, in 1935, the year that President Franklin Roosevelt signed the Wagner Act, less than 1% of trade unionists were African American. While the Wagner act extended basic organizing rights to private sector workers, millions of minorities remained unable to enjoy its protections by the actions of unions themselves. But throughout the second half of the 20th

Century, many unions shed these racist and xenophobic legacies.

In so doing, they opened up their organizations to African Americans eager to escape explicitly racist policies and practices common to many nonunion workplaces. African Americans soon had the highest organization rates of any racial or ethnic group, peaking at more than 40% for African American men and nearly 25% for African American women in the private sector.

These exceptional organization rates helped narrow racial pay disparities by raising African American wages. Had no union decline occurred from the early 1970s on, black-white wage gaps among women would be between 13% and 30% lower, and black males' weekly wages would be an estimated US$50 higher. Meanwhile, many immigrants and their children, echoing pathways taken by newcomers in generations past, such as the predominantly female, predominantly immigrant population of the International Ladies' Garment Workers' Union (ILGWU), used the labor movement as a springboard into the nation's middle class.

Unions' equalizing impact was not limited to the economic realm. A large body of research has found that union membership spurs civic participation among non-elite Americans. Voting, for example, is a practice strongly graded by income and education. More of either and Americans are much more likely to turnout to vote. Unions helped to counteract class-based inequality in political participation, ensuring that elected officials heard the policy desires of millions of non-elite Americans.

WHAT NOW FOR LABOR?

The labor movement now finds itself in a peculiar period.

On the one hand, ongoing attacks by anti-union forces have crippled unions' organizational models in what were labor strongholds, including Wisconsin and Michigan. Many of these attacks have taken dead aim at what remains of labor's real strength: its public sector membership base.

Abetted by recent court decisions, efforts to defund and defang public sector unions are growing in size and sophistication by right wing policymakers and lobbying groups.

Curiously, despite serving as a primary source of votes and finances for the Democratic Party for much of the 20th Century, labor finds itself with few political allies.

On the other hand, unions have enjoyed a series of recent successes at the state and local level. Movements to raise the minimum wage, offer paid sick leave to employees and pressure the largest private sector employer—Walmart—to raise its base compensation have all, of late, succeeded. These victories can be attributed, in part, to labor unions.

Unions provided much of the organizational and financial support that helped deliver these victories to millions of working Americans. Yet none of these wins translate directly into new dues-paying members.

Further successes on behalf of America's working- and middle-class appear limited unless unions discover a means to maintain its funding base. And without a revitalized labor movement, it is likely our inequality levels will remain at record highs.

1. What effect did unionization have on African American workers?

2. What helped cause a decline in unions?

"LABOR UNIONS' DECLINE SINCE THE 1980S HAS GIVEN CORPORATE MANAGEMENT A FREE HAND TO MAKE MASSIVE, PERMANENT LAYOFFS," BY JIWOOK JUNG, FROM THE LONDON SCHOOL OF ECONOMICS US CENTRE, DECEMBER 3, 2015

Until the 1980s most large corporate layoffs meant the temporary suspension of employment, rather than the more permanent downsizing which we know today. In new research which examines nearly 700 layoff announcements over 16 years, Jiwook Jung examines what led to this change in corporate policy. He finds that the decline of industrial unions led what were once temporary layoffs, which were often followed by recall in better economic times, to become permanent. Though labor unions resisted this shift, their decline meant that firm managers were able to gain an upper hand in making decisions about layoffs.

In February, 1993, IBM, the world's largest computer maker, announced that it would order the first layoffs in its then 80-year history. In the face of tougher international and domestic competition, the company had suffered from a steady decline in profitability and slow growth throughout the 1980s; workforce adjustment and cost reduction seemed warranted. Nevertheless, IBM's decision marked a drastic departure from its acclaimed tradition of lifetime employment. Throughout its history, it had prided itself on caring for its employees. Seen in a broader context, however, what was truly remarkable was the fact that the company had managed to avoid layoffs for so long; most of its peers had already accepted the practice as necessary.

Indeed, corporate America had experienced waves of downsizing since the 1980s. And even before the 1980s, firms made layoffs during economic downturns. But the 1980s marked a sea change in the layoff policy of large US companies. Whereas layoff had previously meant *temporary* suspension of employment with an explicit or implicit agreement that laid-off workers would be called back when economic situations improved, it has recently come to mean permanent termination (see Figure 1 below). Moreover, unlike in the past, even healthy, profitable companies have begun to engage in downsizing. For instance, in 1993 Xerox announced its plan to cut 10,000 jobs or nearly 10 percent of its work force, although the company had been consistently profitable before the announcement. Its CEO explained that in order to compete effectively, the company would have to be lean and flexible.

FIGURE 1—TEMPORARY AND PERMANENT LAYOFF ANNOUNCEMENTS

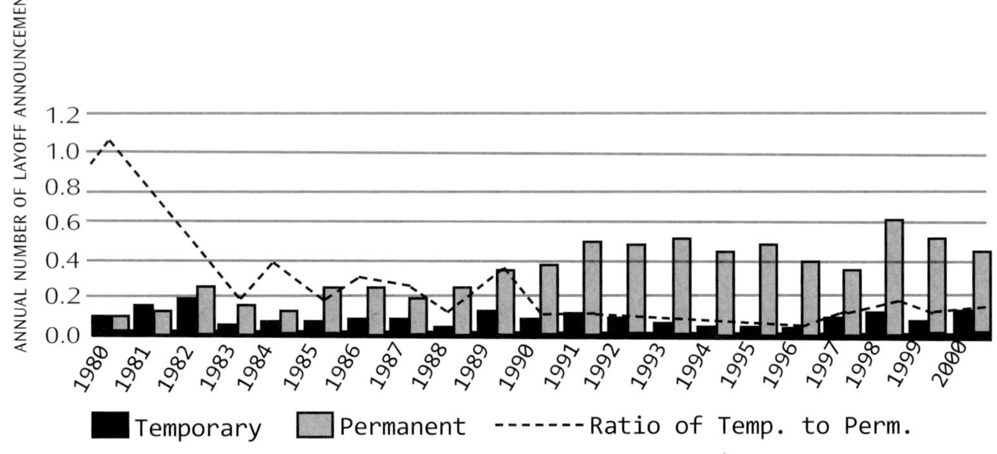

Note: This figure plots the average count of the number of layoff announcements made by 679 large US firms from 1984 to 2000 in a sample constructed by the author.

What can explain this radical shift in layoff policies at large US companies? Factors put forward to explain this phenomenon have included: intensifying market competition, declining manufacturing activities, and technological innovation that has replaced human labor. While these are all important factors, such explanations neglect political-institutional aspects of the shift. In new research, I show that behind this transformation of layoff policies were changing inter-class power relations within large US firms. Several previous studies show that powerful shareholders and top managers promoted permanent layoffs as a strategy to maximize shareholder value—the firm's stock price. These studies, however, do not provide the full picture of inter-class power struggle over layoff policies. While focusing on the role of shareholders and top managers, they overlook how workers and labor unions contested the transformation of layoff policies and how the broader political environment constrained their ability to resist.

In my work, I explore labor unions' resistance to the shift from temporary to permanent layoffs. Apparently, labor unions fiercely resisted, but given their declining political influence it is an open question how effective their resistance was. Industrial unions, especially those in key manufacturing sectors such as automotive and steel, once played a significant role in establishing a set of formal rules and informal norms that induced firms to ensure employees saw their employment security was tied to their reciprocal commitment to the company. Temporary layoffs followed by recall were one such action signaling this commitment. Through this practice, firms adjusted workforce size during economic downturns, while workers remained committed to their original employers.

The industrial unionism that guided employment practices in many large US companies, however, began to fall apart in the late 1970s. As the influence of industrial unionism receded, a new set of principles emerged to reshape the employment policies of US firms. As many firms suffered from a chronic decline in their market share and profitability, new power groups in financial markets, especially large institutional investors (e.g., mutual and public pension funds) began to pressure management to enhance profitability and maximize returns to shareholders. Pressured by institutional investors and also emboldened by the Reagan administration's pro-business stance, firms began to actively engage in massive downsizing in order to maintain, restore, and even boost their stock price. This further weakened the bond between employees and employers.

Despite the changed economic and political circumstances, my statistical analysis of both temporary and permanent layoff announcements made by 679 large US companies from 1984 to 2006 shows that temporary layoffs persisted longer within union strongholds. In other words, firms in highly-unionized sectors were more likely to make temporary layoffs. The analysis also shows that permanent layoffs were suspended under the threat of union strikes. Specifically, the rate of permanent layoff announcements was reduced by 32 percent for firms that experienced a work stoppage. An additional analysis shows that the positive effect of union membership on the rate of temporary layoffs was significantly smaller under the two consecutive Republican administrations in the 1980s and the early 1990s. This result suggests that the pro-business stance of Republican administrations significantly weakened unions' ability to maintain temporary layoffs.

These results show how labor unions, despite their declining political influence, resisted the shift in layoff policies, firstly by negotiating with firms for more reliance on temporary layoffs when workforce adjustment was unavoidable, and secondly by discouraging firms from making permanent layoffs through direct confrontation. But the flipside is that the steady decline in union membership and strike activities gave management a free hand in making layoff decisions. An irony here is that although

US firms engaged in downsizing to achieve greater profits and higher stock price, most studies find that downsizing failed to improve firm profitability. Nevertheless, such disappointing outcomes did not deter firms. Downsizing continued throughout the 1990s. The consequential institutionalization of downsizing suggests that without significant political protection, workers' share of corporate resources (i.e., jobs and wages) is an easy target for firms that seek a quick boost in profits and stock price.

1. How did the decline of labor unions lead to layoffs?

"UNIONS ARE THE WORST LABOR DAY DEAL," BY GARY M. GALLES, FROM THE FOUNDATION FOR ECONOMIC EDUCATION, AUGUST 31, 2017

THEY CERTAINLY WON'T SAVE YOU ANY MONEY.

Every Labor Day, unions repeat assertions of advancing the interests of all workers. But those claims are false. Unions harm most American workers.

PROJECT LABOR AGREEMENTS

Unions use government-delegated powers to restrict competition from other workers, extracting higher wages for their members. But higher wages mean fewer job openings because each worker is more expensive to the employer. That forces workers to move to other jobs, increasing the supply of labor services in non-union employment and reducing wages for all workers in those jobs. With far less than 10 percent of private sector workers in unions, more than 90 percent of them are injured by that exercise of union power.

Other union-backed initiatives also show how unions feather their own nests at the expense of other workers. Among the best examples are Project Labor Agreements (PLAs), such as the one recently adopted in Santa Ana (despite a staff report that estimates that it would increase construction costs by 10-20 percent).

PLAs are agreements negotiated between government bodies and unions (but excluding non-union workers and contractors), establishing in advance the terms and conditions that will be imposed on all workers for designated projects.

PLAs are rationalized as buying labor peace, "leveling the playing field" for competitors, guaranteeing projects are completed on time, holding down costs, increasing quality, and safety, etc. But they advance none of these goals. They restrict competition, raise costs, and pick taxpayers' (i.e., other workers') pockets. As Wharton Professor Herbert Northrup wrote in the *Journal of Labor Research*, PLAs "have little or no economic rationale, nor can they be defended on the grounds of labor peace, enhanced safety, or other reasonable criteria."

PLAs supposedly buy labor peace because unions promise not to engage in disruptive activities. Of course, strikes still hit the San Francisco International Airport expansion project, the largest PLA at the time. Such PLAs punish nonunion workers and contractors, who do not threaten strikes, to buy labor peace from unions who threaten strikes—penalizing the innocent (including taxpayers) to reward the guilty. As the New York Supreme Court described it in the Albany Specialties case, it reflects "capitulation to extortion" by unions.

PLA backers assert they just impose equal labor terms on all project bidders, allowing equal competition. But those "equal" terms are anything but even-handed. As in San Francisco and Santa Ana, all workers on the concerned projects, including non-members, must pay union dues and fees, for which they will receive no benefits. Non-union workers must also contribute to union health and pension funds with nothing in return.

RESTRICTING COMPETITION

Virtually all new workers are forced through union hiring halls and even apprentices are union-controlled. Union wages, work rules, job classifications, and hiring and grievance procedures are mandated, raising costs, particularly for non-union bidders. In 2009, John McGowan estimated that PLAs faced employees of non-union contractors with 20 percent cuts in their take-home pay, while increasing non-union employers' costs by about 25 percent.

PLA terms are so onerous to non-union contractors and workers that most will not even bid on PLA projects (86 percent, in a 1997 survey of non-union contractors in Washington). Bids rise as restrictions eliminate bidders (particularly lower-cost non-union contractors), raising costs for taxpayers. For instance, a 1995 study of the Roswell Park Cancer Institute in New York found that the winning bid without a PLA was 26 percent lower than the one with a PLA.

Such results reinforce the repeated failure of PLAs to demonstrate an increase in either quality or safety, and a 1998 GAO investigation that could document no cost efficiencies from PLAs.

Just as with their other exercises of their unique, government-granted power to restrict competition, PLAs harm other workers both directly and as taxpayers financing public projects.

Rather than living up to union claims, Diana Furchtgott-Roth concluded that a PLA "drives out small businesses from competing for these projects; raises their cost to the taxpayers; and funnels a larger stream of union dues from taxpayers' pockets to union treasuries."

So, if we want to make the workers whose contributions we claim to celebrate on Labor Day better off, we should give them more freedom, rather than subjecting them to so many harmful union impositions.

1. What are project labor agreements (PLAs)?

2. How might PLAs harm economic competition?

"HAVE WE FORGOTTEN THE TRUE MEANING OF LABOR DAY?," BY JAY L. ZAGORSKY, FROM *THE CONVERSATION*, AUGUST 29, 2017

Labor Day is a U.S. national holiday held the first Monday every September. Unlike most U.S. holidays, it is a strange celebration without rituals, except for shopping and barbecuing. For most people it simply marks the last weekend of summer and the start of the school year.

The holiday's founders in the late 1800s envisioned something very different from what the day has become. The founders were looking for two things: a means of unifying union workers and a reduction in work time.

HISTORY OF LABOR DAY

The first Labor Day occurred in 1882 in New York City under the direction of that city's Central Labor Union.

In the 1800s, unions covered only a small fraction of workers and were balkanized and relatively weak. The goal of organizations like the Central Labor Union and more modern-day counterparts like the AFL-CIO was to bring many small unions together to achieve a critical mass and power. The organizers of the first Labor Day were interested in creating an event that brought different types of workers together to meet each other and recognize their common interests.

However, the organizers had a large problem: No government or company recognized the first Monday in September as a day off work. The issue was solved temporarily by declaring a one-day strike in the city. All striking workers were expected to march in a parade and then eat and drink at a giant picnic afterwards.

The *New York Tribune*'s reporter covering the event felt the entire day was like one long political barbecue, with "rather dull speeches."

WHY WAS LABOR DAY INVENTED?

Labor Day came about because workers felt they were spending too many hours and days on the job.

In the 1830s, manufacturing workers were putting in 70-hour weeks on average. Sixty years later, in 1890, hours of work had dropped, although the average manufacturing worker still toiled in a factory 60 hours a week.

These long working hours caused many union organizers to focus on winning a shorter eight-hour work day. They also focused on getting workers more days off, such as the Labor Day holiday, and reducing the workweek to just six days.

These early organizers clearly won since the most recent data show that the average person working in manufacturing is employed for a bit over 40 hours a week and most people work only five days a week.

Surprisingly, many politicians and business owners were actually in favor of giving workers more time off. That's because workers who had no free time were not able to spend their wages on traveling, entertainment or dining out.

As the U.S. economy expanded beyond farming and basic manufacturing in the late 1800s and early 1900s, it became important for businesses to find consumers interested in buying the products and services being produced in ever greater amounts. Shortening the work week was one way of turning the working class into the consuming class.

COMMON MISCONCEPTIONS

The common misconception is that since Labor Day is a national holiday, everyone gets the day off. Nothing could be further from the truth.

While the first Labor Day was created by striking, the idea of a special holiday for workers was easy for politicians to support. It was easy because proclaiming a holiday, like Mother's Day, costs legislators nothing and benefits them by currying favor with voters. In 1887, Oregon, Colorado, Massachusetts, New York and New Jersey all declared a special legal holiday in September to celebrate workers.

Within 12 years, half the states in the country recognized Labor Day as a holiday. It became a national holiday in June 1894 when President Grover Cleveland signed the Labor Day bill into law. While most people interpreted this as recognizing the day as a national vacation, Congress' proclamation covers only federal employees. It is up to each state to declare its own legal holidays.

Moreover, proclaiming any day an official holiday means little, as an official holiday does not require private employers and even some government agencies to give their workers the day off. Many stores are open on Labor Day. Essential government services in protection and transportation continue to function, and even less essential programs like national parks are open. Because not everyone is given time off on Labor Day, union workers as recently as the 1930s were being urged to stage one-day strikes if their employer refused to give them the day off.

In the president's annual Labor Day declaration last year, Obama encouraged Americans "to observe this day with appropriate programs, ceremonies and activities that honor the contributions and resilience of working Americans."

The proclamation, however, does not officially declare that anyone gets time off.

CONTROVERSY: MILITANTS AND FOUNDERS

Today most people in the U.S. think of Labor Day as a noncontroversial holiday.

There is no family drama like at Thanksgiving, no religious issues like at Christmas. However, 100 years ago there was controversy.

The first controversy that people fought over was how militant workers should act on a day designed to honor workers. Communist, Marxist and socialist members of the trade union movement supported May 1 as an international day of demonstrations, street protests and even violence, which continues even today.

More moderate trade union members, however, advocated for a September Labor Day of parades and picnics. In the U.S., picnics, instead of street protests, won the day.

There is also dispute over who suggested the idea. The earliest history from the mid-1930s credits Peter J. McGuire, who founded the New York City Brotherhood of Carpenters and Joiners, in 1881 with suggesting a date that would fall "nearly midway between the Fourth of July and Thanksgiving" that "would publicly show the strength and esprit de corps of the trade and labor organizations."

Later scholarship from the early 1970s makes an excellent case that Matthew Maguire, a representative from the Machinists Union, actually was the founder of Labor Day. However, because Matthew Maguire was seen as too radical, the more moderate Peter McGuire was given the credit.

Who actually came up with the idea will likely never be known, but you can vote online here to express your view.

HAVE WE LOST THE SPIRIT OF LABOR DAY?

Today Labor Day is no longer about trade unionists marching down the street with banners and their tools of trade. Instead, it is a confused holiday with no associated rituals.

The original holiday was meant to handle a problem of long working hours and no time off. Although the battle over these issues would seem to have been won long ago, this issue is starting to come back with a vengeance, not for manufacturing workers but for highly skilled white-collar workers, many of whom are constantly connected to work.

If you work all the time and never really take a vacation, start a new ritual that honors the original spirit of Labor Day. Give yourself the day off. Don't go in to work. Shut off your phone, computer and other electronic devices connecting you to your daily grind. Then go to a barbecue, like the original participants did over a century ago, and celebrate having at least one day off from work during the year!

1. What was the original meaning of Labor Day?

2. How did labor unions affect the workweek?

"LABOR UNIONS CREATE UNEMPLOYMENT: IT'S A FEATURE, NOT A BUG," BY SARAH SKWIRE, FROM THE FOUNDATION FOR ECONOMIC EDUCATION, JUNE 3, 2015

THE LOS ANGELES MINIMUM WAGE FIASCO WAS NO ACCIDENT

Did the labor unions goof, or did they get exactly what they want?

Los Angeles has approved a minimum wage hike to $15 an hour. Some of the biggest supporters of that increase were the labor unions. But now that the increase has been approved, the unions are fighting to exempt union labor from that wage hike.

Over at *Anything Peaceful*, Dan Bier has nicely explained why the unions would do something that seems, at first glance, so nonsensical. But what I want to point out is that this kind of hijinks is not a new invention of 21st century organized labor. Instead, it's pretty much what labor was organized to do. It's a feature, not a bug.

Part of the early reasoning for the minimum wage—which originated as a "family wage" or "living wage"—was its intent to allow a worker to "keep his wife and children out of competition with himself" and presumably to keep all other women out of the workforce as well.

Similarly, the labor movement, from the very beginning, meant to protect organized white male labor from competition against black labor, immigrant labor, female labor, and nonunion labor. There are subtleties to this generalization, of course, and labor historian Ruth Milkman identifies four historical waves of the labor movement that have differing commitments (and a lack thereof) to a more diverse vision of labor rights. But unions—like so many other institutions—work on the "get up and bar the door" principle. Get up as high as you can, and then bar the door behind you against any further entrants who might cut into the goodies you have grabbed for yourself.

Labor union expert Charles Baird notes,

> Unions depend on capture. They try to capture employers by cutting them off from alternative sources of labor; they try to capture workers by eliminating union-free employment alternatives; and they try to capture customers by eliminating union-free producers. Successful capture generates monopoly gains for unions.

Protection is the name of the game.

Unsurprisingly, the unions made sure to be involved when, about 50 years before the 1970s push for an equal rights amendment, there was another push for an ERA in the United States. Written by suffragist leader Alice

Paul, the amendment was an attempt to leverage the newly recognized voting power of women into a policy that guaranteed men and women "shall have equal rights throughout the United States and every place under its jurisdiction." This amendment would have prevented various gender-based inequities that the courts supported at the time—like hugely different hourly wages for male and female workers, limits on the number of hours women could work, limits on when women could work (night shifts were seen as particularly dangerous for women's health and welfare), and limits on the kinds of work women could do.

Reporting on the debates over the ERA in 1924, Doris Stevens noted three main objections to the amendment:

First, there was the familiar plea for gradual, rather than sweeping change.

Second, there were concerns over lost pensions for widows and mothers.

And in Stevens's words,

> The final objection says: Grant political, social, and civil equality to women, but do not give equality to women in industry.... Here lies the heart of the whole controversy. It is not astonishing, but very intelligent indeed, that the battle should center on the point of woman's right to sell her labor on the same terms as man. For unless she is able equally to compete, to earn, to control, and to invest her money, unless in short woman's economic position is made more secure, certainly she cannot establish equality in fact. She will have won merely the shadow of power without essential and authentic substance.

Suffragist Rheta Childe Dorr (in *Good Housekeeping*, of all places. How the mighty have fallen!) pointed out again the logic behind labor's opposition to the equal rights amendment:

> The labor unions are most opposed to this law, for few unions want women to advance in skilled trades. The Women's Trade Union League, controlled and to a large extent supported by the men's unions, opposes it. Of course, the welfare organizations oppose it, for it frees women wage earners from the police power of the old laws. But I pray that public opinion, especially that of the club women, will support it. It's the first law yet proposed that gives working women a man's chance industrially. "No men's labor unions, no leisure class women, no uniformed legislators have a right to govern our lives without our consent," the women declare, and I think they are dead right about it.

Organized labor—founded to ensure the collective right to contract—refused to stand up for the right of individual women to contract. From their point of view, it was only sensible. And, perhaps most importantly, women in organized labor refused to stand up for the women outside the unions.

Organized male *and female* labor's fight against the ERA was at least as much about protectionism as it was about sexism. Maybe more. Women's rights and union activist Ethel M. Smith attended the debates on the ERA to report on it for the *Life and Labor Bulletin*, and found that union workers did not even attempt to gloss over their protectionist agenda:

> Miss Mary Goff of the International Ladies' Garment Workers Union, emphasized the seriousness of the effect upon organized establishments were legal restrictions upon hours of labor removed from the unorganized. "The organized women workers," she said, "need the labor laws to protect them from the competition of the unorganized. Where my union, for instance, may have secured for me a 44-hour week, how long could they maintain it if there were unlimited hours for other workers? Unfortunately, there are hundreds of thousands of unorganized working women in New York who would undoubtedly be working 10 hours a day but for the 9-hour law of New York."

So labor unions excluded women as long as they could, then let in a privileged few and barred the doors behind them. And they continue to use the same tactics today in LA and elsewhere.

How long can they keep it up?

1. Why might labor unions be, by definition, exclusionary?

2. Why were labor unions opposed to the Equal Rights Amendment (ERA)?

"UNIONS PLAY PIVOTAL ROLE MAKING COMPANIES MORE COMPETITIVE," BY PETER LAZES AND ANDREW CROOK, FROM *THE CONVERSATION*, APRIL 10, 2015

When Wisconsin Governor Scott Walker put pen to paper to create America's 25th right-to-work state last month, it became clear that the "labor question" is once again gnawing at the nation's psyche. Do unions bring value to our economy or are they just obstacles to growth?

Walker and others who have led the charge to strangle unions' power justify their actions by saying unions create labor market inefficiencies and fat union bosses. Yet they ignore the vital role they can play in combating inequality, lifting wages, implementing new training programs and rebuilding our economy.

Also lost in the fury in Madison, Wisconsin—and nearly everywhere else labor finds itself under assault—is the underrated but equally significant contribution unionized workplaces make to the resilience of our companies and the quality of our government services.

To weather the storm whipped up by the likes of Walker, organized labor needs to highlight its unique ability to leverage shop floor power to build partnerships with employers and governments. Together, they've successfully rolled out participatory workplace structures that have improved how their organizations are run. If they don't expand these efforts, labor will continue to lose ground to right-to-work laws and other efforts to stifle unions.

SUCCESSFUL UNIONS

The demise of US labor would mean not only the end to resources to help rebuild our economy and reduce inequalities but also the capacity for management to draw on the deep knowledge of frontline staff. That's a partnership that has led to prosperity for both workers and their employers.

During World War II, legendary United Auto Workers leader Walter Reuther knew the value of worker participation in management decisions. Reuther wanted the automakers to convert auto plants so they could manufacture planes and army trucks to help with the war effort. But managers at the Big Three car companies—Ford, General Motors and Chrysler—were initially reluctant to grant the UAW a seat at the table. Reuther persisted until the companies saw the wisdom of his ideas. Record profits and wages followed.

Another example involves Irv Bluestone, chief negotiator for the UAW at GM in the 1970s. He advocated tirelessly to improve "quality of work life" and helped create opportunities so that assembly line workers could help improve the cars they rolled out by working with management to find ways to produce a high-quality, affordable car.

In the 1980s, the UAW was crucial in developing the GM-Toyota California joint venture known as New United Motors Manufacturing (NUMMI), which deployed Japanese-style work teams, extensive training and collaborative labor-management partnerships to bolster productivity and quality far above established GM plants.

This culminated in the historic labor-management partnership that built and ran the Saturn plant in Tennessee, giving rise to a car that competed with the then-dominant Honda Accord. It also provided workers with a voice in decision making, from the layout of the shop floor and the selection of production equipment to the choice of dealerships and suppliers.

While NUMMI and Saturn ultimately closed, victims of the 2008 financial crisis and management intransigence, the lessons learned in autos have spread elsewhere. At heavily unionized Southwest Airlines, for example, labor routinely consults with management on high-level strategic decisions, a structure that helped workers ride out the post-September 11 downturn with zero layoffs.

FORWARD-THINKING CEOS

Instead of fighting their employees, forward-thinking executives and public administrators have partnered with unions to drive growth, improve quality, develop new products, re-train employees and, in the case of the airline industry, made flying safer. Companies like Saturn, Xerox, and Levi Strauss, as well as medical centers such as Montifiore Medical Center and Kaiser Permanente have chosen this high-road strategy.

Employers and unions know how to work together but have often been stymied by short-sighted executives focused exclusively on the share price and rigid work rules such as seniority provisions, promotion rights and job classifications that have denied workers agency and prevented grassroots ideas from being implemented.

In the public sector, where unions remain relatively strong, leaders have long looked beyond collective bargaining and grievance handling and have helped radically reduce costs and improve community services. In education, for instance, Rutgers scholars Saul Rubinstein and John McCarthy have shown that partnerships between teachers' unions, administrators and classroom instructors are a significant predictor of student performance, after controlling for poverty and school type.

At the ABC Unified School District southeast of Los Angeles, which comprises 21,000 students in 30 schools, the authors found that a partnership with the ABC Federation of Teachers improved student achievement. The district consistently scored above the state average on the California Academic Performance Index, despite high percentages of low-income families and English-language learners.

The involvement of rank and file teachers in areas previously the preserve of administrators and school boards taps the endless fountain of knowledge that only they possess.

Perhaps one of the best examples of a long-term worker involvement is in the non-profit healthcare sector, where the Service Employees International Union (SEIU) and Kaiser Permanente have aggressively improved the coordination and quality of patient care while tackling the bloated medical costs that were the target of President Barack Obama's Affordable Care Act.

The labor-management partnership at Kaiser Permanente created unit-based teams to help improve patient satisfaction and strengthen processes to coordinate care and implement a comprehensive electronic medical records systems. Some notable results include reducing unnecessary hospital admissions and tests.

Other healthcare labor-management partnerships in Los Angeles, New York City, Pittsburgh and Seattle have reduced infections, patient falls, re-admissions and unnecessary costs.

LABOR NEEDS TO BROADEN ITS TOOLKIT

Yet these, and many other efforts, often fly under the radar. And partnerships can often go wrong—managers and unions that simply impose reforms without devolving power to worker-led teams are bound to fail. The short-term "gains" of Scott Walker—reduced wages and the elimination of meaningful collective bargaining—become illusory and self destructive as government and corporate leaders realize they have sidelined their most important asset: worker skills and knowledge.

In the face of relentless attacks from short-term profit seekers, labor needs to broaden its toolkit to find concrete ways of strengthening firms and improving public services. It needs to communicate to members that they are more than just an insurance agent. And managers need to stop listening to Walker and think hard about how to embrace unions as vital partners in their company's success.

Band-Aid solutions to manufactured fiscal crises like slashing wages or eroding union security clauses are not sustainable. Instead of denying labor's right to exist, the political class should consider what can be gained by partnering with labor to improve services in the face of cost pressures and cut-throat international competition.

There is now mounting evidence joint labor-management partnerships work can make a difference to improve our economy by enabling workers to have a voice in resolving problems to improve quality of care and services while at same time reduce waste and unneeded costs. But this can only happen if both sides remain committed to the process. The coming years will be a test, not just of the labor movement's metal, but of the commitment of politicians and CEOs to America's best interests.

1. Do you think labor unions contribute to or hinder economic competition? Why or why not?

2. What must labor unions do to "broaden [their] toolkit"?

CHAPTER 2

WHAT THE GOVERNMENT AND POLITICIANS SAY

The government plays an important role in protecting the rights of union members. In the 1930s, Congress passed bills like the Wagner Act, which protected the rights of workers to go on strike. This gave unions bargaining power. The growth of unions can be linked to subsequent strong congressional protections. When politicians and unions disagree, however, it is often over wage increases and pensions for union members. In recent years, politicians have lessened unions' power by passing the Right to Work Act. This act states that unions can't compel workers to join, which then lessens their collective bargaining power. Other amendments to the Wagner Act have lessened the effectiveness of strikes as a labor tactic. With politicians actively working to decrease the power of unions, will the American labor movement create new tactics to put pressure on employers? And will citizens continue to support politicians who do not support unions? This remains to be seen.

"NONPROFITS' STAKE IN CONTROVERSY SURROUNDING PUBLIC SECTOR UNIONS," BY DANIEL STID, FROM THE BRIDGESPAN GROUP, JUNE 30, 2011

The controversy over the role of public sector unions and the compensation and benefits they secure for their members has been one of the most striking aspects of the fiscal shakeout in recent months. This controversy is not likely to end anytime soon. How it plays out will have a significant impact on the resources available to non-profits funded by state and local governments to deliver social services.

The basic dynamics of this issue have been obscured by some high political theater in state capitals. Many Republicans report being shocked—shocked!—to discover that public sector unions' electoral backing of Democratic candidates is reciprocated in staunch support for the compensation, benefits, and bargaining rights of those unions' members. And many Democrats have been in turn shocked—shocked!—to find that Republicans actually have the temerity to seek to undermine the bargaining power and political influence of one of the Democrats' core constituencies. Taking the rhetoric from both sides at face value, you'd almost think that the aggrieved parties have forgotten Mr. Dooley's dictum that politics ain't beanbag. But of course they haven't, which is why they are having this fight.

As the initial smoke from the political conflict clears, we can begin to see that the underlying issues are more complicated—and just what is at stake for nonprofits that rely on government funding. For one thing, it turns out that it is not just red state Republicans that are pushing back on public sector unions. Democratic leaders in decidedly blue states like New York, Maryland, Massachusetts, and Connecticut are as well—with less fireworks and more pragmatism, to be sure, but they are pushing back nonetheless.

They are doing so because—as Willie Sutton said when asked why he robbed banks—that is where the money is. The Center for Budget and Policy Priorities recently estimated that 44 percent of state and local government spending goes to compensation and benefits for public employees. This doesn't take into account the postponed contributions these governments are supposed to be making each year to public employee pension and retiree benefit funds, liabilities that by some estimates now run up to $3 trillion.

The problem is especially acute for local governments, which tend to spend a much higher percentage of their budgets on employee compensation and benefits and supporting their retirees. Manhattan Institute Senior Fellow Steven Malanga noted last week in the *Wall Street Journal* that, for many larger cities, the "the local government pension squeeze" is draining coffers at unfathomable and unsustainable rates. In Providence, RI, for example, 50 percent of the annual tax revenues in the city's budget are now being paid out to the city's pensioners. The *New York Times* ran an illuminating front page story last week on how the electoral influence of public sector unions on politicians of both parties becomes even more intense as you go from the state down to the local level. When the lion's share of available public funding is going to current public employees and retirees by dint of their vested stake and political influence, then the nonprofits delivering services to marginalized populations that are being underwritten by public funding will be left struggling with other hungry claimants over what remains.

These dynamics are calling into question two ostensible truths about public sector unions, one held by the left, the other by the right. Many on the left argue that the fight over public sector pay, benefits, and collective bargaining rights is a struggle that progressives everywhere should rally to join. In this view there are clear and direct lines of justice running from labor's showdowns of yore in places like Harlan and Flint to the current dust-ups in Madison and Trenton.

But if progressives want to stake out their frontlines in this way, then they are going to be dividing their own ranks. The brute fact is that there are clear tradeoffs between pay and benefits for teachers, police, and prison guards on the one hand, and the money available to support services for homeless families, foster youth, and low income seniors on the other. That states have to balance their budgets makes this tradeoff a zero-sum game. Insofar as this leaves nonprofits delivering public services at the behest of the government that they are not being fully reimbursed for, the onus is on the nonprofits to find other, private sources of funds to make ends meet.

But many on the right need to acknowledge that one of their basic beliefs on this topic is quickly becoming something of a myth as well—namely, that public sector unions wield unchecked and thereby illegitimate power relative to their private sector counterparts. Public sector unions, this argument runs, unlike unions bargaining with corporations, can influence and even effectively elect "the management" with whom they negotiate through their political activism and campaign spending. And because state and local governments cannot move their "business" offshore or end up going out of business if labor's demands are too high, public sector unions can and often do press an unfair advantage.

However, as we have seen in the past few months, things are starting to change. State and local governments are running out of money. In the face of this cash crunch, instances of pay and benefits for public employees that are hard to justify will increasingly be questioned, along with the bargaining rights that have given rise to them. Ambitious and determined leaders are challenging and, in some instances, confronting and indeed vilifying public sector unions, wearing their resulting criticism as a political badge of honor. It turns out there is countervailing force to the power of public sector unions, represented by the likes of Governor Andrew Cuomo at one end of the spectrum and Governor Chris Christie at the other. Their position will be strengthened in the years of austerity that lie ahead. Stay tuned!

1. How do union pensions affect city budgets?

2. Why do some politicians challenge unions?

"THE MYTH OF COMPULSORY UNION MEMBERSHIP," BY CHARLES W. BAIRD, FROM THE FOUNDATION FOR ECONOMIC EDUCATION, MARCH 11, 1998

NO AMERICAN WORKER CAN LEGALLY BE FORCED TO BECOME OR REMAIN A UNION MEMBER IN GOOD STANDING IN ANY STATE

Organized labor wants workers to think they can be forced to join a union as a condition of continued employment. The union-employer agreements that accomplish that are called "union security" clauses in collective bargaining pacts.

For example, Weyerhaeuser Paper Co. and the United Paperworkers International Union (UPIU) have a union security clause that requires all maintenance and production employees to "become and remain members of the union in good standing" as a condition of continued employment. It also requires new employees to do the same after a 30-day probationary period. It seems clear: a worker who doesn't join the union will not be employed by Weyerhaeuser. But, as Roland Buzenius proved in a Sixth Federal Circuit Court of Appeals decision on September 8, 1997, that is not what the clause means. If it did mean that, it would be illegal.

It is well known that in the 21 right-to-work states all forms of union security clauses are banned. In those states workers can be forced to have a union (selected by majority vote) represent them, but they cannot be forced to join or pay dues. In the 29 other states—California, for example—union security clauses are permitted, and they are usually worded like the Weyerhaeuser clause. Unions routinely try to use those clauses to dupe workers into thinking that full membership in good standing can be compelled.

Word games have always been a large part of labor-relations law. Section 8(a)3 of the National Labor Relations Act (NLRA) says that it is "an unfair labor practice for an employer by discrimination in regard to hire or tenure of employment . . . to encourage or discourage membership in any labor organization." By itself, that would make union security clauses illegal. However, Section 8(a)3 goes on to say, "provided, that nothing in this Act . . . shall preclude an employer from making an agreement with a labor organization . . . to require as a condition of employment membership therein." In other words, employers cannot encourage membership in a union; they can only compel it. Such is the stuff of laws designed to serve special interests.

The proviso of Section 8(a)3 would seem to make union security clauses that require membership legal. Not so, says the U.S. Supreme Court. In the 1963 case *NLRB v. General Motors Corp.*, the Court said that required membership is limited to its "financial core." That means that the only thing a union can require of the workers it represents is the payment of union dues and initiation fees. No other obligations of membership in good standing can be imposed. In the 1985 case *Pattern Makers' League v. NLRB*, the Court said that any union member in good standing could resign membership at any time for any purpose without giving any notice and become a dues-paying represented worker. Finally, in the 1988 case *Communication Workers of America v. Beck*, the Court said that a worker could be compelled to pay only that portion of union dues and initiation fees used for collective bargaining, contract administration, and grievance procedures. No worker can be compelled to pay dues for such things as politics, lobbying, and union organizing. On average, unions spend only 25 percent of their dues on the three activities for which they may collect forced dues.

So "membership in good standing," as that term is usually interpreted, cannot be compelled in any of the 50 states. All that can be required in the 29 states that have not banned all forms of union security is that workers represented by a union pay partial dues. Any union member paying full dues can resign at will and become a partial-dues, financial-core represented worker. Obviously, unions do not want workers to know this.

This brings us back to Weyerhaeuser and Roland Buzenius, who tried to resign his membership in UPIU. The union ignored his resignation, continued to collect full dues from his paycheck, sent him a new membership card, and said if he resigned he would forfeit his job. National Right to Work Legal Defense Foundation attorneys represented Buzenius against UPIU before the National Labor Relations Board. The NLRB acknowledged Buzenius's rights under the court decisions and ordered the union to stop collecting full dues from him and imposing any other membership requirements on him. It also required the union to post a notice telling all Weyerhaeuser maintenance and production employees that they have the same rights.

However, the NLRB allowed the wording of the union security clause that requires "membership in good standing" to stand. It said that the Supreme Court has never addressed the issue of permissible wording, so any wording agreed to by the employer and the union and consistent with Section 8(a)3, is permissible. Buzenius took the wording issue to the Sixth Circuit Court of Appeals, which on September 8 ruled that the Weyerhaeuser union security clause "leads employees to believe that they must become full-fledged union members as a condition of employment," and since that is "directly at odds with Supreme Court precedent," it must be disallowed.

The Sixth Circuit includes only Kentucky, Michigan, Ohio, and Tennessee. (The issue is moot in Tennessee because it is a right-to-work state.) Until the Supreme Court decides the wording issue, or until Congress codifies the three Supreme Court decisions in amendments to the NLRA, misleading union security clauses will still be allowed in all other non-right-to-work states. But the basic issues are already decided. No American worker can legally be forced to become or remain a union member in good standing in any state.

The trouble is that the Department of Labor refuses to enforce the Supreme Court decisions and allows the AFL-CIO to keep workers in the dark concerning those decisions. This means that workers must file individual cases with the NLRB and the courts to secure their rights.

The National Right to Work Legal Defense Foundation offers free legal representation to workers whose unions refuse to let them resign and become partial-dues, financial-core represented workers. It can be reached on the Internet at www.nrtw.org. An amendment to the NLRA currently under consideration in Congress would extend right-to-work protections to workers in every state. If that were to become law there could be no compulsory union dues for any purpose in any state.

1. The amendment to the NLRA under discussion in this article was not passed. However, it continues to be discussed by politicians and states have passed their own right-to-work laws. Should such an amendment be passed? Why or why not?

2. Why would unions want mandatory membership?

"REMARKS AND A QUESTION-AND-ANSWER SESSION WITH REPORTERS ON THE AIR TRAFFIC CONTROLLERS STRIKE," BY FORMER PRESIDENT RONALD REAGAN, AUGUST 3, 1981

The President. This morning at 7 a.m. the union representing those who man America's air traffic control facilities called a strike. This was the culmination of 7 months of negotiations between the Federal Aviation Administration and the union. At one point in these negotiations agreement was reached and signed by both sides, granting a $40 million increase in salaries and benefits. This is twice what other government employees can expect. It was granted in recognition of the difficulties inherent in the work these people perform. Now, however, the union demands are 17 times what had been agreed to—$681 million. This would impose a tax burden on their fellow citizens which is unacceptable.

I would like to thank the supervisors and controllers who are on the job today, helping to get the nation's air system operating safely. In the New York area, for example, four supervisors were scheduled to report for work, and 17 additionally volunteered. At National Airport a traffic controller told a newsperson he had resigned from the union and reported to work because, "How can I ask my kids to obey the law if I don't?" This is a great tribute to America.

Let me make one thing plain. I respect the right of workers in the private sector to strike. Indeed, as president of my own union, I led the first strike ever called by that union. I guess I'm maybe the first one to ever hold this office who is a lifetime member of an AFL-CIO union. But we cannot compare labor-management relations in the private sector with government. Government cannot close down the assembly line. It has to provide without interruption the protective services which are government's reason for being.

It was in recognition of this that the Congress passed a law forbidding strikes by government employees against the public safety. Let me read the solemn oath taken by each of these employees, a sworn affidavit, when they accepted their jobs: "I am not participating in any strike against the Government of the United States or any agency thereof, and I will not so participate while an employee of the Government of the United States or any agency thereof."

It is for this reason that I must tell those who fail to report for duty this morning they are in violation of the law, and if they do not report for work within 48 hours, they have forfeited their jobs and will be terminated.

Q. Mr. President, are you going to order any union members who violate the law to go to jail?

The President. Well, I have some people around here, and maybe I should refer that question to the Attorney General.

Q. Do you think that they should go to jail, Mr. President, anybody who violates this law?

The President. I told you what I think should be done. They're terminated.

The Attorney General. Well, as the President has said, striking under these circumstances constitutes a violation of the law, and we intend to initiate in appropriate cases criminal proceedings against those who have violated the law.

Q. How quickly will you initiate criminal proceedings, Mr. Attorney General?

The Attorney General. We will initiate those proceedings as soon as we can.

Q. Today?

The Attorney General. The process will be underway probably by noon today.

Q. Are you going to try and fine the union $1 million per day?

The Attorney General. Well, that's the prerogative of the court. In the event that any individuals are found guilty of contempt of a court order, the penalty for that, of course, is imposed by the court.

Q. How much more is the government prepared to offer the union?

The Secretary of Transportation. We think we had a very satisfactory offer on the table. It's twice what other Government employees are going to get—11.4 percent. Their demands were so unreasonable there was no spot to negotiate, when you're talking to somebody 17 times away from where you presently are. We do not plan to increase our offer to the union.

Q. Under no circumstances?

The Secretary of Transportation. As far as I'm concerned, under no circumstance.

Q. Will you continue to meet with them?

The Secretary of Transportation. We will not meet with the union as long as they're on strike. When they're off of strike, and assuming that they are not decertified, we will meet with the union and try to negotiate a satisfactory contract.

Q. Do you have any idea how it's going at the airports around the country?

The Secretary of Transportation. Relatively, it's going quite well. We're operating somewhat in excess of 50 percent capacity. We could increase that. We have determined, until we feel we're in total control of the system, that we will not increase that. Also, as you probably know, we have some rather severe weather in the Midwest, and our first priority is safety.

Q. What can you tell us about possible decertification of the union and impoundment of its strike funds?

The Secretary of Transportation. There has been a court action to impound the strike fund of $3.5 million. We are going before the National Labor Relations Authority this morning and ask for decertification of the union.

Q. When you say that you're not going to increase your offer, are you referring to the original offer or the last offer which you've made? Is that still valid?

The Secretary of Transportation. The last offer we made in present value was exactly the same as the first offer. Mr. Poli (Robert Poli, Professional Air Traffic Controllers Organization) asked me about 11 o'clock last evening if he could phase the increase in over a period of time. For that reason, we phased it in over a longer period of time. It would have given him a larger increase in terms of where he would be when the next negotiations started, but in present value it was the $40 million originally on the table.

Q. Mr. Attorney General, in seeking criminal action against the union leaders, will you seek to put them in jail if they do not order these people back to work?

The Attorney General. Well, we will seek whatever penalty is appropriate under the circumstances in each individual case.

Q. Do you think that is an appropriate circumstance?

The Attorney General. It is certainly one of the penalties that is provided for in the law, and in appropriate cases, we could very well seek that penalty.

Q. What's appropriate?

The Attorney General. Well, that depends upon the fact of each case.

Q. What makes the difference?

Q. Can I go back to my "fine" question? How much would you like to see the union fined every day?

The Attorney General. Well, there's no way to answer that question. We would just have to wait until we get into court, see what the circumstances are, and determine what position we would take in the various cases under the facts as they develop.

Q. But you won't go to court and ask the court for a specific amount?

The Attorney General. Well, I'm sure we will when we reach that point, but there's no way to pick a figure now.

Q. Mr. President, will you delay your trip to California or cancel it if the strike is still on later this week?

The President. If any situation should arise that would require my presence here, naturally I will do that. So, that will be a decision that awaits what's going to happen. May I just—because I have to be back in there for another appointment—may I just say one thing on top of this? With all this talk of penalties and everything else, I hope that you'll emphasize, again, the possibility of termination, because I believe that there are a great many of those people—and they're fine people—who have been swept up in this and probably have not really considered the result—the fact that they had taken an oath, the fact that this is now in violation of the law, as that one supervisor referred to with regard to his children. And I am hoping that they will in a sense remove themselves from the lawbreaker situation by returning to their posts.

I have no way to know whether this had been conveyed to them by their union leaders, who had been informed that this would be the result of a strike.

Q. Your deadline is 7 o'clock Wednesday morning for them to return to work?

The President. Forty-eight hours.

The Secretary of Transportation. It's 11 o'clock Wednesday morning.

Q. Mr. President, why have you taken such strong action as your first action? Why not some lesser action at this point?

The President. What lesser action can there be? The law is very explicit. They are violating the law. And as I say, we called this to the attention of their leadership. Whether this was conveyed to the membership before they voted to strike, I don't know. But this is one of the reasons why there can be no further negotiation while this situation continues. You can't sit and negotiate with a union that's in violation of the law.

The Secretary of Transportation. And their oath.

The President. And their oath.

Q. Are you more likely to proceed in the criminal direction toward the leadership than the rank and file, Mr. President?

The President. Well, that again is not for me to answer.

Q. Mr. Secretary, what can you tell us about the possible use of military air controllers—how many, how quickly can they get on the job?

The Secretary of Transportation. In answer to the previous question, we will move both civil and criminal, probably more civil than criminal, and we now have papers in the U.S. attorneys offices, under the Attorney General, in about 20 locations around the country where would be involved two or three principal people.

As far as the military personnel are concerned, they are going to fundamentally be backup to the supervisory personnel. We had 150 on the job, supposedly, about a half-hour ago. We're going to increase that to somewhere between 700 and 850.

Q. Mr. Secretary, are you ready to hire other people should these other people not return?

The Secretary of Transportation. Yes, we will, and we hope we do not reach that point. Again as the President said, we're hoping these people come back to work. They do a fine job. If that does not take place, we have a training school, as you know. We will be advertising. We have a number of applicants right now. There's a waiting list in terms of people that want to be controllers, and we'll start retraining and reorganize the entire FAA traffic controller group.

Q. Just to clarify, is your deadline 7 a.m. Wednesday or 11 o'clock?

The Secretary of Transportation. It's 11 a.m. Wednesday. The President said 48 hours, and that would be 48 hours.

Q. If you actually fire these people, won't it put your air traffic control system in a hole for years to come, since you can't just cook up a controller in—[inaudible]?

The Secretary of Transportation. That obviously depends on how many return to work. Right now we're able to operate the system. In some areas, we've been very gratified by the support we've received. In other areas, we've been disappointed. And until I see the numbers, there's no way I can answer that question.

Q. Mr. Lewis, did you tell the union leadership when you were talking to them that their members would be fired if they went out on strike?

The Secretary of Transportation. I told Mr. Poli yesterday that the President gave me three instructions in terms of the firmness of the negotiations: one is there would be no amnesty; the second there would be no negotiations during the strike; and third is that if they went on strike, these people would no longer be government employees.

Q. Mr. Secretary, you said no negotiations. What about informal meetings of any kind with Mr. Poli?

The Secretary of Transportation. We will have no meetings until the strike is terminated with the union.

Q. Have you served Poli at this point? Has he been served by the Attorney General?

The Attorney General. In the civil action that was filed this morning, the service was made on the attorney for the union, and the court has determined that that was appropriate service on all of the officers of the union.

Q. My previous question about whether you're going to take a harder line on the leadership than rank and file in terms of any criminal prosecution, can you give us an **answer on that?**

The Attorney General. No, I can't answer that except to say that each case will be investigated on its own merits, and action will be taken as appropriate in each of those cases.

Q. Mr. Lewis, do you know how many applications for controller jobs you have on file now?

The Secretary of Transportation. I do not know. I'm going to check when I get back. I am aware there's a waiting list, and I do not have the figure. If you care to have that, you can call our office, and we'll tell you. Also, we'll be advertising and recruiting people for this job if necessary.

Q. Mr. Secretary, how long are you prepared to hold out if there's a partial but not complete strike?

The Secretary of Transportation. I think the President made it very clear that as of 48 hours from now, if the people are not back on the job, they will not be government employees at any time in the future.

Q. How long are you prepared to run the air controller system—[inaudible]?

The Secretary of Transportation. For years, if we have to.

Q. How long does it take to train a new controller, from the waiting list?

The Secretary of Transportation. It varies; it depends on the type of center they're going to be in. For someone to start in the system and work through the more minor office types of control situations till they get to, let's say, a Chicago or a Washington National, it takes about 3 years. So in this case, what we'll have to do if some of the major metropolitan areas are shut down or a considerable portion is shut down, we'll be bringing people in from other areas that are qualified and then start bringing people through the training schools in the smaller cities and smaller airports.

Q. Mr. Secretary, have you definitely made your final offer to the union?

The Secretary of Transportation. Yes, we have.

Q. Thank you.

Note: The President read the statement to reporters at 10:55 a.m. in the Rose Garden at the White House.

1. Why did former President Ronald Reagan oppose the air traffic controllers' demands?

2. Why did Reagan believe some workers should not be allowed to strike?

"WORKERS ARE NEVER REQUIRED TO JOIN UNIONS," BY DEAN BAKER, FROM THE CENTER FOR ECONOMIC POLICY RESEARCH, APRIL 22, 2011

The *NYT* wrongly told readers that a bill approved by the New Hampshire legislature would, "disallow collective bargaining agreements that require employees to join a labor union." It is already the case that collective bargaining agreements cannot require employees to join a labor union.

Under current New Hampshire law, collective bargaining agreements can require workers to pay representation fees to a union. National labor law requires that a union represent all workers who are in a bargaining unit regardless of whether or not they opt to join the union.

This means that non-members not only get the same wages and benefits as union members, but the union is also required to represent non-members in any conflict with the employer covered by the contract. For example, if a non-member is faced with an improper dismissal the union is obligated to provide them with the same representation as a union member.

The new bill passed by the New Hampshire legislature effectively guarantees non-union members the right to get union representation without paying for it (representation without taxation). It denies workers the freedom of contract that they currently enjoy, which would allow them to require that everyone who benefits from union representation has to share in the cost of union representation.

1. Should unions be required to bargain on behalf of non-union workers? Why or why not?

2. Should workers be required to pay union dues? Why or why not?

"NATIONAL LABOR RELATIONS ACT," BY THE US CONGRESS, FROM THE NATIONAL LABOR RELATIONS BOARD

Congress enacted the National Labor Relations Act ("NLRA") in 1935 to protect the rights of employees and employers, to encourage collective bargaining, and to curtail certain private sector labor and management practices, which can harm the general welfare of workers, businesses and the U.S. economy.

NATIONAL LABOR RELATIONS ACT

Also cited NLRA or the Act; 29 U.S.C. §§ 151-169

[Title 29, Chapter 7, Subchapter II, United States Code]

FINDINGS AND POLICIES

Section 1.[§151.] The denial by some employers of the right of employees to organize and the refusal by some employers to accept the procedure of collective bargaining lead to strikes and other forms of industrial strife or unrest, which have the intent or the necessary effect of burdening or obstructing commerce by (a) impairing the efficiency, safety, or operation of the instrumentalities of commerce; (b) occurring in the current of commerce; (c) materially affecting, restraining, or controlling the flow of raw materials or manufactured or processed goods from or into the channels of commerce, or the prices of such materials or goods in commerce; or (d) causing diminution of employment and wages in such volume as substantially to impair or disrupt the market for goods flowing from or into the channels of commerce.

The inequality of bargaining power between employees who do not possess full freedom of association or actual liberty of contract and employers who are organized in the corporate or other forms of ownership association substantially burdens and affects the flow of commerce, and tends to aggravate recurrent business depressions, by depressing wage rates and the purchasing power of wage earners in industry and by preventing the stabilization of competitive wage rates and working conditions within and between industries.

Experience has proved that protection by law of the right of employees to organize and bargain collectively safeguards commerce from injury, impairment, or interruption, and promotes the flow of commerce by removing certain recognized sources of industrial strife and unrest, by encouraging practices fundamental to the friendly adjustment of industrial disputes arising out of differences as to wages, hours, or other working conditions, and by restoring equality of bargaining power between employers and employees.

Experience has further demonstrated that certain practices by some labor organizations, their officers, and members have the intent or the necessary effect of burdening or obstructing commerce by preventing the free flow of goods in such commerce through strikes and other forms of industrial unrest or through concerted activities which impair the interest of the public in the free flow of such commerce. The elimination of such practices is a necessary condition to the assurance of the rights herein guaranteed

It is declared to be the policy of the United States to eliminate the causes of certain substantial obstructions to the free flow of commerce and to mitigate and eliminate these obstructions when they have occurred by encouraging the practice and procedure of collective bargaining and by protecting the exercise by workers of full freedom of association, self- organization, and designation of representatives of their own choosing, for the purpose of negotiating the terms and conditions of their employment or other mutual aid or protection.

DEFINITIONS

Sec. 2. [§152.] When used in this Act [subchapter]—

(1) The term "person" includes one or more individuals, labor organizations, partnerships, associations, corporations, legal representatives, trustees, trustees in cases under title 11 of the United States Code [under title 11], or receivers.

(2) The term "employer" includes any person acting as an agent of an employer, directly or

indirectly, but shall not include the United States or any wholly owned Government corporation, or any Federal Reserve Bank, or any State or political subdivision thereof, or any person subject to the Railway Labor Act [45 U.S.C. § 151 et seq.], as amended from time to time, or any labor organization (other than when acting as an employer), or anyone acting in the capacity of officer or agent of such labor organization.

[Pub. L. 93-360, § 1(a), July 26, 1974, 88 Stat. 395, deleted the phrase "or any corporation or association operating a hospital, if no part of the net earnings inures to the benefit of any private shareholder or individual" from the definition of "employer."]

(3) The term "employee" shall include any employee, and shall not be limited to the employees of a particular employer, unless the Act [this subchapter] explicitly states otherwise, and shall include any individual whose work has ceased as a consequence of, or in connection with, any current labor dispute or because of any unfair labor practice, and who has not obtained any other regular and substantially equivalent employment, but shall not include any individual employed as an agricultural laborer, or in the domestic service of any family or person at his home, or any individual employed by his parent or spouse, or any individual having the status of an independent contractor, or any individual employed as a supervisor, or any individual employed by an employer subject to the Railway Labor Act [45

U.S.C. § 151 et seq.], as amended from time to time, or by any other person who is not an employer as herein defined.

(4) The term "representatives" includes any individual or labor organization.

(5) The term "labor organization" means any organization of any kind, or any agency or employee representation committee or plan, in which employees participate and which exists for the purpose, in whole or in part, of dealing with employers concerning grievances, labor disputes, wages, rates of pay, hours of employment, or conditions of work.

(6) The term "commerce" means trade, traffic, commerce, transportation, or communication among the several States, or between the District of Columbia or any Territory of the United States and any State or other Territory, or between any foreign country and any State, Territory, or the District of Columbia, or within the District of Columbia or any Territory, or between points in the same State but through any other State or any Territory or the District of Columbia or any foreign country.

(7) The term "affecting commerce" means in commerce, or burdening or obstructing commerce or the free flow of commerce, or having led or tending to lead to a labor dispute burdening or obstructing commerce or the free flow of commerce.

(8) The term "unfair labor practice" means any unfair labor practice listed in section 8 [section 158 of this title].

(9) The term "labor dispute" includes any controversy concerning terms, tenure or conditions of employment, or concerning the association or representation of persons in negotiating, fixing, maintaining, changing, or seeking to arrange terms or conditions of employment, regardless of whether the disputants stand in the proximate relation of employer and employee.

(10) The term "National Labor Relations Board" means the National Labor Relations Board provided for in section 3 of this Act [section 153 of this title].

(11) The term "supervisor" means any individual having authority, in the interest of the employer, to hire, transfer, suspend, lay off, recall, promote, discharge, assign, reward, or discipline other employees, or responsibly to direct them, or to adjust their grievances, or effectively to recommend such action, if in connection with the foregoing the exercise of such authority is not of a merely routine or clerical nature, but requires the use of independent judgment.

(12) The term "professional employee" means--

(a) any employee engaged in work (i) predominantly intellectual and varied in character as opposed to routine mental, manual, mechanical, or physical work; (ii) involving the consistent exercise of discretion and judgment in its performance; (iii) of such a character that the output produced or the result accomplished cannot be standardized in relation to a given period of time; (iv) requiring knowledge of an advanced type in a field of science or learning customarily acquired by a prolonged course of specialized intellectual instruction and study in an institution of higher learning or a hospital, as distinguished from a general academic education or from an apprenticeship or from training in the performance of routine mental, manual, or physical processes; or

(b) any employee, who (i) has completed the courses of specialized intellectual instruction and study described in clause (iv) of paragraph (a), and (ii) is performing related work under the supervision of a professional person to qualify himself to become a professional employee as defined in paragraph (a).

(13) In determining whether any person is acting as an "agent" of another person so as to make such other person responsible for his acts, the question of whether the specific acts performed were actually authorized or subsequently ratified shall not be controlling.

(14) The term "health care institution" shall include any hospital, convalescent hospital, health maintenance organization, health clinic, nursing home, extended care facility, or other institution devoted to the care of sick, infirm, or aged person.

1. Why does the Wagner Act protect workers' right to strike?

2. How do strikes help protect the rights of workers?

"UNIONS LOSE THEIR GAMBLE ON BELTWAY POLITICS," BY MATTHEW CUNNINGHAM-COOK, FROM *WAGING NONVIOLENCE*, FEBRUARY 10, 2013

On January 25, labor unions in the United States were dealt a major blow. The D.C. Circuit Appeals Court—the second most powerful court in the country and one closely aligned with the Supreme Court—handed down a decision declaring President Barack Obama's recess appointments to the National Labor Relations Board invalid, which will likely nullify the rules and decisions of the NLRB in the past two years. Because the Senate is unlikely to approve any appointments in the next two years, labor unions are left with effectively no legal recourse against employers for the foreseeable future.

Unions spent hundreds of millions of dollars on both the 2008 and 2012 elections, and securing a functional National Labor Relations Board was one of the main reasons. The board, established in 1935 to mediate and arbitrate labor disputes, is the central federal agency that enforces laws related to unions, with its stated goal being to promote collective bargaining. Over the past few years, the NLRB has taken some significant actions, most notably preventing Boeing from punishing its workers by shifting work from Washington state to South Carolina, where laws are less amenable to organized labor. It also announced a new rule requiring employers to have a poster in every workplace that informs workers of their rights to collectively bargain under the National Labor Relations Act, just as they are required to inform employees of their rights under the Civil Rights Act of 1964, the Fair Labor Standards Act, the Occupational Safety and Health Act, and the Americans with Disabilities Act. Now these gains are in jeopardy.

While the NLRB has generally served to protect labor organizing, it can also sanction unions for violations of often technical and restrictive labor laws—most notably Section 8(b) of the National Labor Relations Act, which among other things prevents unions from targeting employers for longer than 60 days. This resulted, for instance, in the recent NLRB-arbited settlement between the union-affiliated worker center OUR Walmart and Walmart stores, which requires OUR Walmart to stop picketing for two months.

According to labor lawyer Joe Burns, this settlement demonstrates that the NLRB never should have been viewed as a panacea for the labor movement. "It's pretty clear even before this decision that the NLRB doesn't provide meaningful protection for workers," he said. "It's crystal clear that we can't rely on the NLRB, so any illusions that we could—this should dispel them."

With a federal judiciary that draws almost exclusively from the ranks of corporate lawyers and prosecutors—two of the most anti-labor realms of the legal profession—one must wonder about whether even a normally functioning board could uphold its mandate to promote collective bargaining.

Burns added, "The question we need to ask as a labor movement is this: should we rely on this process or do we have to use some other tactics?"

The National Labor Relations Act was initially passed in 1934 in the face of a colossal strike wave that included citywide general strikes in San Francisco and Minneapolis. The goal was progressive—to promote collective bargaining—but at the same time it was a compromise made by a capitalist class determined to achieve a semblance of industrial peace. By having a state-sponsored framework for negotiating working conditions, employers would be able to avoid debilitating strikes and enjoy greater productivity.

Union membership as a percentage of the workforce today, however, is the lowest in 76 years—almost as long ago as when the law was passed—and the conditions of the historic compromise that created the NLRB aren't in place anymore, thanks to a confluence of trends: increased automation, foreign trade, growing employer resistance, and the decline of pro-labor institutions like the NLRB and the Department of Labor. But the question now becomes what unions need to do to—at the very least—stop hemorrhaging workers.

Many unions have adopted new strategies in the face of this decline, with both the Walmart campaign and a broader strike-first strategy. These approaches are less dependent than more traditional ones on structures like the NLRB. But almost everyone in organized labor agrees that a non-functioning NLRB is still bad for unions and workers. Chris Rhomberg, a professor at Fordham University and the author of the 2012 book *The Broken Table: The Detroit News Strike and the Decline of American Labor*, insists that the National Labor Relations Act still offers important protections for workers, despite the restrictions it places on unions.

"I think the Walmart settlement highlights that the NLRA is really contradictory now," he said. "The people who attempt to carry out the goal of the law—the promotion of collective bargaining—find themselves very constricted." But, he added, "I think it's also true that we can't pretend that it's not there."

Kate Bronfenbrenner, director of Labor Education Research at the School of Industrial and Labor Relations at Cornell, believes that the onus is on unions to get the NLRB functioning again.

"Labor's response should be to keep on aggressively organizing without the board," she said. "If unions file unfair labor practice charges every time they see them, and keep striking and doing the kind of the things where the employer wants to get injunctive relief, employers and Senate Republicans will realize that they need the NLRB. There needs to be a lack of industrial peace."

Chris Townsend, an international representative for the United Electrical Workers union, suggests that it's not just Republicans who pose an obstacle in Washington. He asked, "Are we also going to include the question of whether or not we are going to reevaluate our relationship with the Democratic Party? Or are we going to realize that the Democratic Party is too compromised, so we think about developing an independent political movement?"

It is true, the Democratic Senate failed to take up the limited labor-law reform advocated by unions in 2008 and 2009—the Employee Free Choice Act—and the reason that Obama had to make recess appointments to the NLRB in the first place is that Democratic Sen. Harry Reid failed to move the appointments to the floor. Ostensibly, the Democrats' rationale was Republican intransigence, but the Democrats also had a 20-seat supermajority in that body. Meanwhile, Democrats in

Congress have failed to release nary a peep of opposition to the administration's "Race to the Top" program, which has led to significant restrictions in the ability of teachers and school employees to collectively bargain.

For now, most unions seem to be awaiting the results of the inevitable Supreme Court appeal of the January 25 decision. But in in light of the court's 7-2 anti-labor ruling in June 2012, it seems unlikely that it will be sympathetic. Joe Burns thinks that organized labor should use this opportunity to expand the ground for new tactics—and potentially for an entirely new modus operandi in the labor movement.

"I think unions are coming up with creative strategies to try and address the decline of unionism," he said. "But it's hard to see a strategy that doesn't in some form involve violating labor law. I think that's the big question we as a broader labor movement have to address."

1. How do amendments to the National Labor Relations Act make strikes less effective?

2. Why are union leaders calling for new tactics?

"FUTURE OF UNIONS IN BALANCE AS TRUMP PREPARES TO RESHAPE NATIONAL LABOR BOARD," BY NICOLE HALLETT, FROM *THE CONVERSATION*, JUNE 12, 2017

Last October, employees of the Elderwood Nursing Home in Grand Island, New York, voted to unionize after years of dealing with short staffing, stagnant wages and problems with management. Six months later, the company has yet to come to the bargaining table, claiming that there are unresolved legal questions about whether licensed practical nurses can be part of the Service Employees International Union (SEIU).

Yale University has recently come under criticism for making a similar decision. Despite a February vote to unionize by graduate students in eight departments, Yale has so far resisted calls to begin the bargaining process. Instead, it has appealed the decision to certify the election and is refusing to bargain until the appeal is decided.

Elderwood and Yale could hardly be more different. Yale is a world-class Ivy League bastion of higher education. Elderwood is a medium-sized elder care company that operates nursing home facilities in New York, Pennsylvania and Rhode Island. Yet both have made the strategic decision to not recognize the right of their employees to unionize. Why?

My research on the decline of the labor movement suggests a reason: Employers are counting on a changing of the guard at the National Labor Relations Board (NLRB).

The NLRB is the administrative agency that is tasked with enforcing the National Labor Relations Act, the federal statute that gives employees the right to unionize and collectively bargain. The NLRB consists of five members who are appointed to five-year terms by the president upon the advice and consent of the Senate.

Right now, there are two vacancies on the board that President Donald Trump will fill. Once the Senate confirms President Trump's nominees, Republicans will control the board for the first time since 2007.

The background of the three candidates reportedly under consideration suggests that the board will in fact be much friendlier to business interests under the Trump administration. One of the potential nominees, Doug Seaton, has made a career of being a "union-buster," the term used to describe a consultant brought in by employers to beat a unionization campaign. Another, William Emanuel, is a partner at Littler Mendelson, one of the largest and most successful anti-labor law firms in the country. Less is known about the third potential candidate, Marvin Kaplan, but his history as a Republican staffer suggests he may also represent employers' interests.

Many observers assume that this new board will overturn many Obama-era precedents that favored unions. These precedents include questions such as how to define bargaining units, at issue at both Yale and Elderwood.

But the new board could go even further and roll back pro-union decisions dating back decades. This could be devastating to already weakened unions. With private sector union membership hovering at a dismal 6.4 percent—down from about 17 percent in 1983—nothing short of the end of the labor movement could be at stake.

HOW POLITICS INTRUDED ON THE NLRB

The composition of the NLRB is important because most claims regarding the right to organize and collectively bargain are decided by the agency.

Unlike other employment statutes, such as Title VII and the Fair Labor Standards Act, individuals and unions cannot file claims in federal court and instead must participate in the administrative process set up by the National Labor Relations Act. While aggrieved parties can appeal board rulings to federal appeals courts, judges grant a high degree of deference to NLRB decisions.

In other words, three board members—a bare majority of the board—have an enormous ability to influence and shape American labor policy.

Given the amount of power these three individuals can wield, it is no wonder that the NLRB has become highly politicized in the decades since its creation in the 1930s. Ironically, the board was originally established as a way to try to insulate labor policy from political influences.

The drafters of the labor act believed that the federal courts were hostile to labor rights and would chip away at the protections in a way that would be bad for unions. Instead, the board has become a political battlefield for the two parties who hold very different views about labor policy.

This politicization came to a head during the Obama administration, when it became impossible to confirm anyone to serve on the NLRB. In response, Obama appointed several members using his recess appointment power, which allows the president to avoid Senate confirmation of nominees when Congress is in recess.

Employers challenged the move, and the Supreme Court eventually invalidated the recess appointments as executive overreach in *NLRB v. Noel Canning*. After the decision, Obama and the Senate finally agreed on five members that were confirmed. This new board, with a Democratic majority, then decided many of the precedents that employers hope the new members will overturn.

FLAWS IN THE NATIONAL LABOR RELATIONS ACT

So what will happen if Elderwood and Yale bet wrong and lose their appeals in front of the new Republican-controlled board?

In all likelihood, not much. The board process is long and cumbersome. It often takes years from the filing of a charge for failure to bargain to the board's decision. In the meantime, employers hope that unions will have turnover in their membership, become disorganized and lose support.

Moreover, the penalties available under the National Labor Relations Act are weak. If an employer is found to have violated the act, the board can issue a "cease-and-desist" letter and require the employer to post a notice promising not to engage in further violations. These penalties hardly encourage employers to comply with their obligations, especially when they have so much to gain from obstructing attempts to unionize and collectively bargain.

If the labor movement is to survive, the National Labor Relations Act needs to be reformed to fix these problems. Instead, a few years of a Republican-controlled NLRB could be organized labor's death knell.

1. In September 2018, President Trump elected William Emmanuel to the National Labor Relations Board. From the background given in this article, how might this appointment affect labor relations in the United States?

CHAPTER 3

WHAT THE COURTS SAY

The courts, like politicians, can be favorable or unfavorable toward unions. The courts goal in deciding cases between workers and corporations should be to protect the rights and safety of all citizens. They must also interpret the law when new disputes arise. Many judges are appointed by politicians, which lead many to question how impartial they can truly be. When citizens cannot agree about the rights of unions they also turn to the courts to settle labor disputes—like whether or not unions should be allowed to collect dues from all employees. Many union members find recent court cases allowing workers to leave unions but still benefit from their negotiations to be harmful to unions. The rise of "Right to Work" laws in many states have been linked to the decline of unions in those areas. Recently, workers in the fast food industry in particular are learning how court cases surrounding franchising and ownership will affect their attempts to unionize.

"RIGHT-TO-WORK'S RAPID SPREAD IS CREATING MORE UNION FREE RIDERS," BY ROLAND ZULLO, FROM *THE CONVERSATION*, APRIL 3, 2015

An effort to weaken organized labor is sweeping the Midwest, a region with a rich history of union activism.

The strategy takes advantage of a curious provision of US labor law, section 14 (b). It allows states to pass laws that prohibit unions from negotiating the collection of union dues with employers and, more specifically, from compelling workers covered by the bargaining agreement to pay them as a condition of employment.

Under labor law, employees that do not pay dues enjoy the same wages, benefits and protections as those who do. A labor union that discriminates against someone covered by the contract (and who doesn't pay dues) is liable to a duty of fair representation lawsuit.

Corporations call these laws "right-to-work" (RTW). Unions prefer the term "right-to-freeload" (RTF).

Wisconsin last month became the latest (and 25th) state to pass legislation that allows union-covered workers to refrain from paying dues. Legislators in Illinois, Missouri, Kentucky and New Mexico are agitating to following suit.

What do these laws mean for organized labor?

WHAT RTW ISN'T ABOUT

First, let us begin by anticipating and then dismissing several pretexts. RTW is not about granting workers the freedom to associate, as supporters argue. If that were the case, then RTW advocates would approach the minority union concept, keenly argued by Charles Morris in *The Blue Eagle at Work: Reclaiming Democratic Rights in the American Workplace*, with equal zeal.

Morris explains that the intent of the original labor law was to promote collective bargaining by compelling employers to negotiate with groups of workers on behalf of members only, even if they did not constitute at least 50% of employees. Silence on this issue from right-to-work supporters undermines the credibility of the "freedom to associate" motive.

RTW is also not about making labor unions more responsive to workers by allowing them to withhold dues payments. The very same objective could be achieved by allowing union objectors to remit the equivalent of union dues to an agreed-upon charity, enabling workers to register dissatisfaction with a union without giving them a financial incentive to do so. Hence, the objection would genuinely reflect ideology or religious concerns, and not free-rider opportunism.

However, the American Legislative Council (ALEC)-sponsored legislation sweeping the nation expressly prohibits any requirement to "pay to any charity or other third party, in lieu of such payments, any amount equivalent to or a pro-rata portion of dues, fees, assessments, or other charges regularly required of members of a labor organization."

ALEC is a group of conservative state legislators that crafts "model" legislation and lobbies like-minded politicians to pass the bills, as has been the case with right-to-work.

WHAT RTW DOES

One way to understand the real intent of RTW is to imagine what would happen to the public services in one's town, city or state if the payment of taxes were voluntary. How long would our public schools, libraries, sanitation systems, water facilities, parks and so forth function if taxes were optional?

Charging fees would be impermissible, because persons that refuse to pay tax would have an equal right to the schools, libraries, garbage collection, water, etc, as those that do pay. Just like RTW, the services would have to remain equally accessible to tax payers as well as tax deadbeats. Public services as we know them would collapse.

All collective endeavors require resources to achieve their goals. Labor unions represent working persons at their place of employment through collective bargaining. Organized labor also has an admirable history of fighting on behalf of non-union workers through political advocacy on issues such as workplace safety, minimum wage and public health insurance. The obvious intent of the ALEC-funded RTW effort is to burden the union movement's pursuit of these goals by making it difficult to acquire financial resources.

LABOR FREE RIDERS

Evidence of a RTW burden is beginning to appear in state-level statistics.

The graph below provides trends lines for the union free rider percentages in Illinois, Indiana, Michigan and Wisconsin. The free rider percentage is the percent of persons in the state that are covered by a collective bargaining agreement but are not union members. The estimates are from the Current Population Survey administered by the Bureau of Labor Statistics.

UNION FREE RIDER PERCENTAGES FOR U.S. MID-WEST STATES, 2004-2014

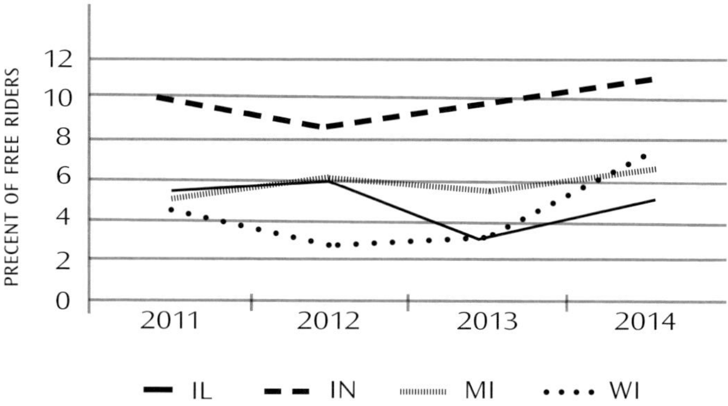

The top line is Indiana, which passed RTW in 2012. The dashed line at the bottom is Michigan, which passed RTW in late 2012, effective 2013. Both states show a gain in the percentages of free riders following the passage of RTW laws.

The growth in free riders for Michigan would have been even more dramatic had RTW applied immediately to all collective bargaining agreements. Prior to the law, many unions across the state signed binding letters of intent with their employers to extend union security provisions. As these letters expire, the RTW burden will predictably increase.

Wisconsin (dotted line) displays an upward trend in free ridership, although quite gradual by comparison with Indiana and Michigan. The trend in Wisconsin might be attributable to the evisceration of collective bargaining rights for public employees in 2011. The Midwest state that has experienced little change in bargaining law, Illinois (solid line), has a free rider rate from 4% to 6%, and no discernible trend over the period.

ELITE ARROGANCE BACK IN VOGUE?

It is important to not only acknowledge these trends but to understand the context that gives rise to RTW, or any other anti-worker policy. What does RTW symbolize?

On a political level, the expansion of RTW is symptomatic of the resurgent influence of corporate control over political affairs. Advocates for RTW, as agents of the corporate class, evidently have enough resources to convince persons to vote to undermine one of the few social institutions that advance the interests of working persons.

Observing these events brings to mind the quip attributed to the 19th-century railroad baron, Jay Gould, during an earlier era of great inequality: "I can hire one half of the working class to kill the other half." Elite arrogance is back in vogue.

1. What is the freedom to associate?

2. Why do unions collect dues?

EXCERPT FROM *AMERICAN FEDERATION OF LABOR, ET AL. V. AMERICAN SASH & DOOR COMPANY ET AL.*, FROM THE US SUPREME COURT, JANUARY 3, 1949

No. 27. Argued: November 8-10, 1948. --- Decided: January 3, 1949.

This case is here on appeal from the Supreme Court of Arizona under § 237 of the Judicial Code as amended, 28 U.S.C. 344, 28 U.S.C.A. § 344 (now § 1257). It involves the constitutional validity of the following amendment to the Arizona Constitution, adopted at the 1946 general election:

> 'No person shall be denied the opportunity to obtain or retain employment because of non-membership in a labor organization, nor shall the State or any subdivision thereof, or any corporation, individual or association of any kind enter into any agreement, written or oral, which excludes any person from employment or continuation of employment because of non-membership in a labor organization.' Laws Ariz.1947, p. 399.

The Supreme Court of Arizona sustained the amendment as constitutional against the contentions that it 'deprived the union appellants of rights guaranteed under the First Amendment and protected against invasion by the states under the Fourteenth Amendment to the United States Constitution'; that it impaired the obligations of existing contracts in violation of Art. I, § 10, of the United States Constitution; and that it deprived appellants of due process of law, and denied them equal protection of the laws contrary to the Fourteenth Amendment. All of these questions properly reserved in the state court, were decided against the appellants by the State Supreme Court.[1] The same questions raised in the state court are presented here.

For reasons given in two other cases decided today we reject the appellants' contentions that the Arizona amendment denies them freedom of speech, assembly or petition, impairs the obligation of their contracts, or deprives them of due process of law. Lincoln Federal Labor Union No. 19129, *American Federation of Labor v. Northwestern Iron & Metal Co.*, and *Whitaker v. State of North Carolina*, 335 U.S. 525, 69 S.Ct. 251. A difference between the Arizona amendment and the amendment and statute considered in the Nebraska and North Carolina cases has made it necessary for us to give separate consideration to the contention in this case that the Arizona amendment denies appellants equal protection of the laws.

The language of the Arizona amendment prohibits employment discrimination against non-union workers, but it does not prohibit discrimination against union workers. It is argued that a failure to provide the same protection for union workers as that provided for non-union workers places the union workers at a disadvantage, thus denying unions and their members the equal protection of Arizona's laws.

Although the Arizona amendment does not itself expressly prohibit discrimination against union workers, that state has not left unions and union members without protection from discrimination on account of union membership. Prior to passage of this constitutional amendment, Arizona made it a misdemeanor for any person to coerce a worker to make a contract 'not to join or become a member of any labor organization' as a condition of getting or holding a job in Arizona. A.C.A.1939, § 43-1608. A section of the Arizona code made every such contract (generally known as a 'yellow dog contract') void and unenforceable.[2] Similarly, the Arizona constitutional amendment makes void and unenforceable contracts under which an employer agrees to discriminate against non-union workers. Statutes implementing the amendment have provided as sanctions for its enforcement relief by injunction and suits for damages for discrimination practiced in violation of the amendment. [3] Whether the same kind of sanctions would be afforded a union worker against whom an employer discriminated is not made clear by the opinion of the State Supreme Court in this case. But assuming that Arizona courts would not afford a remedy by injunction or suit for damages, we are unable to find any indication that Arizona's amendment and statutes are weighted on the side of non-union as against union workers. We are satisfied that Arizona has attempted both in the anti-yellow-dog-contract law and in the anti-discrimination constitutional amendment to strike at what were considered evils, to strike where those evils were most felt, and to strike in a manner that would effectively suppress the evils.

In *National Labor Relations Board v. Jones & Laughlin Steel Corp.*, 301 U.S. 1, 57 S.Ct. 615, 81 L.Ed. 893, 108 A.L.R. 1352, this Court considered a challenge to the National Labor Relations Act on the ground that it applied restraints against employers but did not apply similar restraints against wrongful conduct by employees. We there pointed out, 301 U.S. at page 46, 57 S.Ct. at page 628, the general rule that 'legislative authority, exerted within its proper field, need not embrace all the evils within its reach.' And concerning state laws we have said that the existence of evils against which the law should afford protection and the relative need of different groups for that protection 'is a matter for the legislative judgment.' *West Coast Hotel Co. v. Parrish*, 300 U.S. 379, 400, 57 S.Ct. 578, 586, 81 L.Ed. 703, 108 A.L.R. 1330. We cannot say that the Arizona amendment has denied appellants equal protection of the laws.

Affirmed.

Mr. Justice MURPHY, dissents.

For concurring opinions of Mr. Justice FRANKFURTER and Mr. Justice RUTLEDGE, see 335 U.S. 538, 69 S.Ct. 260.

[...]

Mr. Justice RUTLEDGE, concurring.

I concur in the Court's judgment in No. 34, *Whitaker v. North Carolina*. The appellants were convicted under a warrant which charged only, in effect, that they had violated the statute 'by executing a written agreement or contract' for a closed or union shop.[1] There was neither charge nor evidence that the employer, after the statute became effective, had refused employment to any person because he was not a member of a union. The charge, therefore, and the conviction were limited to the making of the contract. No other provision of the statute is now involved, as the state's attorney general conceded, indeed as he strongly urged, in the argument here. As against the constitutional objections raised to this application of the statute, I agree that the legislature has power to proscribe the making of such contracts, and accordingly join in the judgment affirming the convictions.

In No. 27, *American Federation of Labor v. American Sash & Door Company*, and in No. 47, *Lincoln Federal Labor Union v. Northwestern Iron & Metal Company*, as against the constitutional questions now raised, I am also in agreement with the Court's decision, but subject to the following reservation. Because no strike has been involved in any of the states of fact, no question has been presented in any of these cases immediately involving the right to strike or concerning the effect of the Thirteenth Amendment. Yet the issues so closely approach touching that right as it exists or may exist under that Amendment that the possible effect of the decisions upon it hardly can be ignored.[2] Strikes have been called throughout union history in defense of the right of union members not to work with nonunion men. If today's decision should be construed to permit a state to foreclose that right by making illegal the concerted refusal of union members to work with nonunion workers, and more especially if the decision should be taken as going so far as to permit a state to enjoin such a strike,[3] I should want a complete and thorough reargument of these cases before deciding so momentous a question.

But the right to prohibit contracts for union security is one thing. The right to force union members to work with nonunion workers is entirely another. Because of this difference, I expressly reserve judgment upon the latter question until it is squarely and inescapably presented. Although this reservation is not made expressly by the Court, I do not understand its opinion to foreclose this question.

1. Should it be illegal for union members to refuse to work with non-union members?

2. How could forcing union members to work with non-union members lessen the effectiveness of strikes?

"INTERNATIONAL COVENANT ON ECONOMIC, SOCIAL AND CULTURAL RIGHTS," BY THE UNITED NATIONS, DECEMBER 16, 1966

ADOPTED AND OPENED FOR SIGNATURE, RATIFICATION AND ACCESSION BY GENERAL ASSEMBLY RESOLUTION 2200A (XXI) OF 16 DECEMBER 1966 ENTRY INTO FORCE 3 JANUARY 1976, IN ACCORDANCE WITH ARTICLE 27

PREAMBLE

The States Parties to the present Covenant,

Considering that, in accordance with the principles proclaimed in the Charter of the United Nations, recognition of the inherent dignity and of the equal and inalienable rights of all members of the human family is the foundation of freedom, justice and peace in the world,

Recognizing that these rights derive from the inherent dignity of the human person,

Recognizing that, in accordance with the Universal Declaration of Human Rights, the ideal of free human beings enjoying freedom from fear and want can only be achieved if conditions are created whereby everyone may enjoy his economic, social and cultural rights, as well as his civil and political rights,

Considering the obligation of States under the Charter of the United Nations to promote universal respect for, and observance of, human rights and freedoms,

Realizing that the individual, having duties to other individuals and to the community to which he belongs, is under a responsibility to strive for the promotion and observance of the rights recognized in the present Covenant,

Agree upon the following articles:

PART I

ARTICLE 1

1. All peoples have the right of self-determination. By virtue of that right they freely determine their political status and freely pursue their economic, social and cultural development.

2. All peoples may, for their own ends, freely dispose of their natural wealth and resources without prejudice to any obligations arising out of international economic co-operation, based upon the principle of mutual benefit, and international law. In no case may a people be deprived of its own means of subsistence.

3. The States Parties to the present Covenant, including those having responsibility for the administration of Non-Self-Governing and Trust Territories, shall promote the realization of the right of self-determination, and shall respect that right, in conformity with the provisions of the Charter of the United Nations.

PART II

ARTICLE 2

1. Each State Party to the present Covenant undertakes to take steps, individually and through international assistance and co-operation, especially economic and technical, to the maximum of its available resources, with a view to achieving progressively the full realization of the rights recognized in the present Covenant by all appropriate means, including particularly the adoption of legislative measures.

2. The States Parties to the present Covenant undertake to guarantee that the rights enunciated in the present Covenant will be exercised without discrimination of any kind as to race, colour, sex, language, religion, political or other opinion, national or social origin, property, birth or other status.

3. Developing countries, with due regard to human rights and their national economy, may determine to what extent they would guarantee the economic rights recognized in the present Covenant to non-nationals.

ARTICLE 3

The States Parties to the present Covenant undertake to ensure the equal right of men and women to the enjoyment of all economic, social and cultural rights set forth in the present Covenant.

ARTICLE 4

The States Parties to the present Covenant recognize that, in the enjoyment of those rights provided by the State in conformity with the present Covenant, the State may subject such rights only to such limitations as are determined by law only in so far as this may be compatible with the nature of these rights and solely for the purpose of promoting the general welfare in a democratic society.

ARTICLE 5

1. Nothing in the present Covenant may be interpreted as implying for any State, group or person any right to engage in any activity or to perform any act aimed at the destruction of any of the rights or freedoms recognized herein, or at their limitation to a greater extent than is provided for in the present Covenant.
2. No restriction upon or derogation from any of the fundamental human rights recognized or existing in any country in virtue of law, conventions, regulations or custom shall be admitted on the pretext that the present Covenant does not recognize such rights or that it recognizes them to a lesser extent.

PART III

ARTICLE 6

1. The States Parties to the present Covenant recognize the right to work, which includes the right of everyone to the opportunity to gain his living by work which he freely chooses or accepts, and will take appropriate steps to safeguard this right.

2. The steps to be taken by a State Party to the present Covenant to achieve the full realization of this right shall include technical and vocational guidance and training programmes, policies and techniques to achieve steady economic, social and cultural development and full and productive employment under conditions safeguarding fundamental political and economic freedoms to the individual.

ARTICLE 7

The States Parties to the present Covenant recognize the right of everyone to the enjoyment of just and favourable conditions of work which ensure, in particular:

(a) Remuneration which provides all workers, as a minimum, with:

(i) Fair wages and equal remuneration for work of equal value without distinction of any kind, in particular women being guaranteed conditions of work not inferior to those enjoyed by men, with equal pay for equal work;

(ii) A decent living for themselves and their families in accordance with the provisions of the present Covenant;

(b) Safe and healthy working conditions;

(c) Equal opportunity for everyone to be promoted in his employment to an appropriate higher level, subject to no considerations other than those of seniority and competence;

(d) Rest, leisure and reasonable limitation of working hours and periodic holidays with pay, as well as remuneration for public holidays

ARTICLE 8

1. The States Parties to the present Covenant undertake to ensure:

   (a) The right of everyone to form trade unions and join the trade union of his choice, subject only to the rules of the organization concerned, for the promotion and protection of his economic and social interests. No restrictions may be placed on the exercise of this right other than those prescribed by law and which are necessary in a democratic society in the interests of national security or public order or for the protection of the rights and freedoms of others;

   (b) The right of trade unions to establish national federations or confederations and the right of the latter to form or join international trade union organizations;

(c) The right of trade unions to function freely subject to no limitations other than those prescribed by law and which are necessary in a democratic society in the interests of national security or public order or for the protection of the rights and freedoms of others;

(d) The right to strike, provided that it is exercised in conformity with the laws of the particular country.

2. This article shall not prevent the imposition of lawful restrictions on the exercise of these rights by members of the armed forces or of the police or of the administration of the State.

3. Nothing in this article shall authorize States Parties to the International Labour Organisation Convention of 1948 concerning Freedom of Association and Protection of the Right to Organize to take legislative measures which would prejudice, or apply the law in such a manner as would prejudice, the guarantees provided for in that Convention.

ARTICLE 9

The States Parties to the present Covenant recognize the right of everyone to social security, including social insurance.

ARTICLE 10

The States Parties to the present Covenant recognize that:

1. The widest possible protection and assistance should

be accorded to the family, which is the natural and fundamental group unit of society, particularly for its establishment and while it is responsible for the care and education of dependent children. Marriage must be entered into with the free consent of the intending spouses.

2. Special protection should be accorded to mothers during a reasonable period before and after childbirth. During such period working mothers should be accorded paid leave or leave with adequate social security benefits.

3. Special measures of protection and assistance should be taken on behalf of all children and young persons without any discrimination for reasons of parentage or other conditions. Children and young persons should be protected from economic and social exploitation. Their employment in work harmful to their morals or health or dangerous to life or likely to hamper their normal development should be punishable by law. States should also set age limits below which the paid employment of child labour should be prohibited and punishable by law.

ARTICLE 11

1. The States Parties to the present Covenant recognize the right of everyone to an adequate standard of living for himself and his family, including adequate food, clothing and housing, and to the continuous improvement of living conditions. The States Parties will take

appropriate steps to ensure the realization of this right, recognizing to this effect the essential importance of international co-operation based on free consent.

2. The States Parties to the present Covenant, recognizing the fundamental right of everyone to be free from hunger, shall take, individually and through international co-operation, the measures, including specific programmes, which are needed:

   (a) To improve methods of production, conservation and distribution of food by making full use of technical and scientific knowledge, by disseminating knowledge of the principles of nutrition and by developing or reforming agrarian systems in such a way as to achieve the most efficient development and utilization of natural resources;

   (b) Taking into account the problems of both food-importing and food-exporting countries, to ensure an equitable distribution of world food supplies in relation to need.

ARTICLE 12

1. The States Parties to the present Covenant recognize the right of everyone to the enjoyment of the highest attainable standard of physical and mental health.

2. The steps to be taken by the States Parties to the present Covenant to achieve the full realization of this right shall include those necessary for:

(a) The provision for the reduction of the stillbirth-rate and of infant mortality and for the healthy development of the child;

(b) The improvement of all aspects of environmental and industrial hygiene;

(c) The prevention, treatment and control of epidemic, endemic, occupational and other diseases;

(d) The creation of conditions which would assure to all medical service and medical attention in the event of sickness.

ARTICLE 13

1. The States Parties to the present Covenant recognize the right of everyone to education. They agree that education shall be directed to the full development of the human personality and the sense of its dignity, and shall strengthen the respect for human rights and fundamental freedoms. They further agree that education shall enable all persons to participate effectively in a free society, promote understanding, tolerance and friendship among all nations and all racial, ethnic or religious groups, and further the activities of the United Nations for the maintenance of peace.

2. The States Parties to the present Covenant recognize that, with a view to achieving the full realization of this right:

(a) Primary education shall be compulsory and available free to all;

(b) Secondary education in its different forms, including technical and vocational secondary education, shall be made generally available and accessible to all by every appropriate means, and in particular by the progressive introduction of free education;

(c) Higher education shall be made equally accessible to all, on the basis of capacity, by every appropriate means, and in particular by the progressive introduction of free education;

(d) Fundamental education shall be encouraged or intensified as far as possible for those persons who have not received or completed the whole period of their primary education;

(e) The development of a system of schools at all levels shall be actively pursued, an adequate fellowship system shall be established, and the material conditions of teaching staff shall be continuously improved.

3. The States Parties to the present Covenant undertake to have respect for the liberty of parents and, when applicable, legal guardians to choose for their children schools, other than those established by the public authorities, which conform to such minimum educational standards as may be laid down or approved by the State and to ensure the religious and moral education of their children in conformity with their own convictions.

4. No part of this article shall be construed so as to interfere with the liberty of individuals and bodies to establish and direct educational institutions, subject

always to the observance of the principles set forth in paragraph I of this article and to the requirement that the education given in such institutions shall conform to such minimum standards as may be laid down by the State.

ARTICLE 14

Each State Party to the present Covenant which, at the time of becoming a Party, has not been able to secure in its metropolitan territory or other territories under its jurisdiction compulsory primary education, free of charge, undertakes, within two years, to work out and adopt a detailed plan of action for the progressive implementation, within a reasonable number of years, to be fixed in the plan, of the principle of compulsory education free of charge for all.

ARTICLE 15

1. The States Parties to the present Covenant recognize the right of everyone:

   (a) To take part in cultural life;

   (b) To enjoy the benefits of scientific progress and its applications;

   (c) To benefit from the protection of the moral and material interests resulting from any scientific, literary or artistic production of which he is the author.

2. The steps to be taken by the States Parties to the present Covenant to achieve the full realization of this right

shall include those necessary for the conservation, the development and the diffusion of science and culture.

3. The States Parties to the present Covenant undertake to respect the freedom indispensable for scientific research and creative activity.

4. The States Parties to the present Covenant recognize the benefits to be derived from the encouragement and development of international contacts and co-operation in the scientific and cultural fields.

1. Why does the United Nations (UN) protect the right of workers to form unions?

"WHY IS COLLECTIVE BARGAINING A CONSTITUTIONAL QUESTION?," BY HOWARD SAMUELS, FROM NYCONSTITUTION.ORG: A PROJECT OF THE HOWARD SAMUELS NEW YORK POLICY CENTER, INC.

The right of workers to organize and select representatives to collectively bargain for them was guaranteed by the Bill of Rights in the 1938 New York State Constitution.

WHY COLLECTIVE BARGAINING MATTERS

The introductory provision in section 17 of the New York State Bill of Rights, providing that human labor is not a commodity or an article of commerce was a major social policy pronouncement arising out of the labor movement. It had originated with the federal Clayton Act and was intended to protect labor from antitrust conspiracy charges, and while some felt it was unnecessary to include in the Constitution, it was incorporated because it presented an ennobling view of people that was worth emphasizing.

The right of employees to collectively bargain through representatives of their own choosing had already been recognized in the courts, but by not defining employees as public or private this provision maintained the existing exclusion from collective bargaining for public employees, as well as those of religious, nonprofit and charitable institutions. This is significant because the Supreme Court over the years had interpreted the right to bargain collectively as including the right to strike, which was a right the 1938 Constitutional Convention could not have agreed upon.

It was only in 1967, with the enactment of the Taylor Law, that public employees gained the right to collectively bargain through representatives of their choosing, but without the right to strike.

In both Ohio and Wisconsin, which have recently attempted to restrict collective bargaining rights, such rights are statutory and can be changed by the legislature. Unlike the New York State Constitution, the constitution in those states contains no mention of collective bargaining.

1. What is collective bargaining?

2. What effect did the Taylor Law have on unions?

"THE FUTURE OF THE LOW-WAGE WORKER MOVEMENT MAY DEPEND ON AN UNHERALDED NYC LAW," BY MAX ZAHN, FROM *WAGING NONVIOLENCE*, AUGUST 2, 2017

Flavia Cabral doesn't equivocate. She joined the fast food worker movement, she said, for a single reason: to put her daughter through college.

Cabral, 53, of the Bronx, earned $7.25 per hour at McDonald's when she stood alongside coworkers in her first single-day strike four years ago. Over 10 strikes later, she makes $12 per hour, thanks to a statewide minimum wage hike that will gradually elevate her pay to $15 by the end of 2018.

Still, her goal remains out of reach.

"I don't have enough savings for my daughter to finish college," she said. "I want her to graduate."

Cabral's predicament is emblematic of one facing the Fight for $15: how to move beyond its titular demand to address other barriers that are keeping fast food workers from a middle class life. These obstacles include insufficient hours, non-union workplaces and crippling expenses like housing, health insurance and college education.

Fight for $15 won an important victory on one of these fronts in late-May when the New York City Council passed a bundle of laws that guarantee predictable schedules and require restaurants to offer additional hours to current workers before hiring new employees. Similar laws have been passed in cities like Seattle and San Francisco.

A less heralded law within the package of New York City reforms, however, may hold the future of the fast food movement—and, if successful, will offer an inroad to unionizing the 42 percent of American workers who make less than $15 per hour.

The ordinance allows fast food workers to join a new type of labor organization, which will advocate for workers throughout the industry and sustain itself through dues deducted voluntarily from workers' paychecks.

It is, some say, the kernel of what could become a sector-wide fast food union—the movement's holy grail.

In order to begin deducting dues from workers' paychecks, the new organization, Fast Food Justice, needs to sign up at least 500 workers and it aims to do so by the time the law goes into effect at the end of November. Labor leaders in other cities and low-wage sectors are watching closely to find out if the model is worth replicating.

"There is a lot riding on this experiment," said Janice Fine, a professor of labor studies at Rutgers University. "It's incredibly important but we don't know if it will work."

When it began in New York City in 2012, the Fight for $15 made two demands on behalf of fast food workers: a $15 per hour minimum wage and union representation. Due to a headline-grabbing campaign of single-day strikes, the former has enjoyed increasing popularity and policy success. Last year California and New York each passed a statewide $15 minimum wage; cities like Minneapolis and Seattle have done so, too. When introduced in April, a U.S. Senate bill calling for a $15 minimum wage garnered support from 24 senators, including progressive stalwarts like Bernie Sanders and centrist members like Charles Schumer and Cory Booker.

The union demand, on the other hand, has stalled.

The urgency behind this demand springs not only from a need for worker gains but movement stability. Since its inception, Fight for $15 has received the entirety of its funding from dues-paying members of the Service Employees International Union, or SEIU. But the 2-million-member labor organization will cut overall spending by 10 percent this year and 30 percent in 2018 as it braces for Trump era political battles and an unfavorable Supreme Court decision in *Janus v. AFSCME*—a relitigation of Friedrichs that could substantially reduce membership in public sector locals. As of last year, the union had spent $70 million on the fast food campaign. It has yet to reap a penny in dues from an industry worker.

"There's a problem of institutionalization and sustainability," said Nelson Lichtenstein, a labor historian and professor at the University of California, Santa Barbara. "An independent source of income would give backbone."

Hector Figueroa, president of the powerful SEIU local 32BJ, said the "leadership of SEIU is committed to Fight for $15," though he acknowledged that everyone will be affected by the cuts, including the fast food campaign. "We don't feel particularly disturbed or concerned about financial decisions for the union. We take this fight very seriously."

That said, Figueroa acknowledged that gaining union representation remains a goal of the campaign. Cabral agreed. "We want to fight for $15 *and* a union," she said.

Obstacles to unionization for the 3.67 million fast food workers nationwide, or even the 65,000 in New York City, are daunting. Rapid employee turnover coupled with the industry's franchise model renders traditional store-by-store organizing difficult. The National Labor Relations Board allowed for an alternative in 2015 when it loosened its standard for whether a corporation, say McDonald's, can be considered a joint employer along with its franchises, opening the door for a union of McDonald's employees nationwide. But a Trump-appointed board is almost certain to reverse the NLRB decision.

"Joint employer status will soon be out the door," Figueroa said. "We're trying to adapt to continue the campaign under a different set of circumstances."

Figueroa pointed to a successful 32BJ drive last year that forced multiple contractors at airports in New York and New Jersey to recognize a union of 8,000 security and maintenance workers.

"With public support and with workers continuing to raise issues, franchisors recognize it's a sensible decision to support workers at the store level," he said. "This is a brave new world."

Even so, Figueroa conceded that the fast food campaign faces challenges of a different magnitude. "These are mega companies," he said. "They exist everywhere."

It raises the question: can Fast Food Justice enable the first step toward a concrete fast food worker organization?

Fast Food Justice works like this: If at least 500 workers sign up to join the organization, it can begin receiving contributions from workers who voluntarily deduct money from their paychecks. Employers, then, are responsible for transferring the payments to Fast Food Justice. It's as simple as that.

The group plans to function like a sector-specific community organization, offering education on worker rights and advocating on issues that confront the fast food workforce, which is disproportionately black and Latino.

"We want to take on community issues," said Shantel Walker, a Papa John's employee and leader of the Fight for $15. "We want to support immigration reform, and we need affordable housing and an end to police brutality."

"When you talk to workers they don't just raise issues in the workplace, a policy advocacy organization can make a difference for them at the New York City Council to effect change in different ways and provide outreach and education," echoed Tsedeye Gebreselassie, a senior staff attorney at the National Employment Law Project and a board member of Fast Food Justice.

This advocacy model is hardly unprecedented. Membership-based groups like the Retail Action Project and the Taxi Workers Alliance, which represents 19,000 taxi drivers in New York City, lack collective bargaining rights but achieve gains on the job through political mobilization off it. The Taxi Workers Alliance, for instance, organized its largely immigrant membership to carry out a ride boycott at JFK airport in January in response to the Trump travel ban.

Fast Food Justice will borrow from these forebears but will operate under an entirely new funding mechanism. Other groups ask workers to pay a monthly or yearly fee, but deducting voluntary dues directly from paychecks will allow the organization to secure regular contributions from workers who may lack bank accounts or debit cards.

"Once you have dues check off, it's much easier if you're automatically opted in and then don't have to think about it again," Lichtenstein said.

More importantly, it centers dues payment within each member's store. Fast Food Justice will benefit from sector-wide breadth and the massive potential membership base it provides. But unlike its peers, the group will anchor membership in worker's relationship to a specific store and boss.

"It definitely creates both a structure and funding base to organize strong workplace-based organization," said Karen Scharf, the executive director of a state-wide community organization called Citizen Action and a New York State co-chair for the Working Families Party. "It really is the important next step for the fast food movement to be organizing the shops."

Stuart Applebaum, the president of the Retail, Wholesale and Department Store Union applauded the organization as a "positive step."

"People who had no way of expressing their voices before will now have an opportunity," he said. "I would hope that this would eventually lead to unionization."

"You can begin to have shop stewards in every store," Lichtenstein said, likening the organization to a right-to-work union before catching himself.

"The more we like it, the more it looks like a union; and the more it looks like a union, the easier it is to attack it legally," he said.

Legal anxieties, in this case, aren't illustrative of an embattled left crying wolf. They're warranted. A lawsuit could claim that the ordinance preempts the federal National Labor Relations Act, which retains jurisdiction over what constitutes a labor organization, Lichtenstein said. A passage within the New York City law explicitly states that it does not allow for contributions to a labor organization, as defined by the NLRA. But a restaurant trade group or conservative organization may argue otherwise.

Ironically, the prospect puts Fast Food Justice and 32BJ officials in the position of arguing that the new organization doesn't resemble a union, while critics argue that it does.

"It doesn't get into issues of pay terminations or grievances of the job," Figueroa said. "These are very distinct functions of labor unions that the organization won't touch."

Gabresellasie added: "This is not a union; it's not trying to bargain with one employer or one workplace."

Kevin Dugan, a regional director with the New York State Restaurant Association, a trade organization that opposed the law, disagreed.

Asked if he thinks new organization amounts to a union, he said, "it's hard not to when you have groups like 32BJ filing for non-profit designations. Let the Department of Labor decide whether this is skirting certain regulations or not."

Despite the saber rattling, Dugan acknowledged that neither the New York State Restaurant Association nor its nationwide umbrella organization is currently planning to challenge the law in court.

Of course such plans may change or another adversarial group may step in to fill the void.

For now, though, the only obstacle preventing this organization from collecting worker dues is the minimum 500 sign-ups necessary to trigger payments. The organization would like to reach that number by the time the law goes into effect at the end of November. At first glance the task may appear easy, considering the group can draw from a base of 65,000 workers. But Fast Food Justice is gearing up for a massive organizing campaign to reach this initial goal.

"I think it's a good test," Fine said. "If they can't get there, it's really problematic."

The organization has already begun hiring organizers and signing up workers, Fast Food Justice spokesperson Eliza Margarita Bates said.

"Reaching out to 500 individuals is not a quick process—that's organizing, right?" Gabreselassie said. "It's not just going into one workplace; it's going across the city."

Ultimately, she said, the task won't "be that strenuous. We have time to do it and do it well."

But there's reason to be skeptical, as the organizing challenges that have dogged Fight for $15 are still at play.

While the organization achieved a $15 minimum wage hike in New York State through a massive multi-year mobilization, turnout at strike-day rallies was made up predominantly of community members. The first fast food strike, in November 2012, saw an estimated 200 workers in New York City walk off the job and, based on news reports, the movement peaked at 400 workers turning out to strike. One can fairly assume a degree of overestimation in such numbers, which were self-reported by Fight for $15. Participants did risk retaliation from management, but they were not asked to contribute money.

"Once fast food leaders talk to coworkers they could find interest is not there," Figueroa said. "We don't know if it will work."

Those very leaders are more sanguine. "This is how we built Fight for $15," Walker said. "We organized ourselves."

"We're still fighting for whatever it takes," Cabral added. "We are unstoppable."

The single-day strike tactic began in New York before spreading to hundreds of other cities and drawing in thousands of low-wage workers. A similar fate may await this organizational model, which could begin its expansion with statewide legislation in Albany. "I would not be surprised in the future if that is an option," Figueroa said. "The conditions for fast food workers are similar everywhere."

Lichtenstein said this approach to organizing workers could extend beyond fast food. "It's obviously a model if it works for all sorts of low-wage industries, which are roughly the same," he said. "It's true in retail and big box stores—the next place it goes for sure."

Appelbaum disagreed, saying, "what we're seeing is that in fast food this legislation may be the right way to go. That does not mean it's the right way to go in other industries." He noted the success of RWDSU organizing retail workers in New York City, like the breakthrough at Zara, where over 1,000 workers unionized last year. "In fast food, where there is no real organization at this point anywhere, the model that was proposed makes sense," he said.

"The only place retail organizing has vaguely succeeded is New York," Lichtenstein rebutted. "In most places, it's zero on non-grocery retail and big boxes. In California or other liberal states one could see an ordinance passed that created such a mechanism for retail in the whole state."

The spread of this organizational model will likely depend on the political winds in large municipalities and states considering adoption.

"This shouldn't be a left-wing or right-wing thing," Fine said. "Certainly in progressive cities it's probably going to be a lot easier. It shouldn't be, but that's the reality."

The growth of the model may prove a bellwether of the struggle between pro-business Trumpism and the labor resistance—both within and outside the Democratic party—that has emerged in the aftermath of November's unexpected election.

But Cabral said the movement will endure, regardless of who's president.

"Trump or not Trump, we're going to keep fighting for what we workers deserve: a decent life and a decent salary."

1. What are the Fight for 15's goals?

2. Why is forming a union of fast food workers difficult?

CHAPTER 4

WHAT ADVOCACY ORGANIZATIONS SAY

Unions may be on the decline in the United States but union organizers are working to change that. The power of labor movements comes from their numbers. This is why many organizers are beginning to focus on growing the size of unions. Today many unions are focused on issues like raising the minimum wage and preventing wage theft. For many years unions, like the Service Employees International Union (SEIU), donated large sums of money to politicians who supported union workers. However, these relationships have not proved helpful in terms of union friendly legislation. Some organizers, like those of the Red Party, believe it is time for unions to return to more direct action like strikes and work slowdowns. Part of the job of organizers is to educate new workers on the history of unions and the wisdom behind their tactics. This kind of education leads to new members and more powerful unions.

"LOW-WAGE WORKERS, TOP-DOWN UNIONS," BY PETER RUGH, FROM *WAGING NONVIOLENCE*, SEPTEMBER 30, 2013

August 29 was a typically cool, wet summer day in downtown Seattle. "We support you!" cried the crowd of 30 or so gathered outside Specialty's Café, their voices reverberating off the glass facades of adjacent downtown buildings. To remain open, the restaurant had been forced to call in extra staff. Six of its workers had joined the national fast-food workers' strike that day to demand $15 per hour and a union.

The crowd in front of Specialty's was distinctly of the type able to attend an anti-corporate demonstration in the middle of a workday—young and mostly white, trying to act as allies. Their chants were not those of workers with a grievance so much as those of outsiders seeking to connect with Speciality's labor force inside.

After much encouragement from the crowd, a young man named Jonathan Hargrove walked out of the café and met a euphoric reception. "I didn't know there was a strike going on," he said. "I've always known workers were trampled on, but I didn't know there was a picket today."

As they spread across the United States, "Fight for 15" actions like this one have spurred a debate over what constitutes a living wage, casting a spotlight on working families in an economy where the odds are increasingly stacked against them. Beginning with fast-food restaurant strikes in New York City last November, the campaign has gone national in large part due to the backing of the Service Employees International Union. The effort has been a public-relations success for SEIU and for the labor movement generally, which otherwise appears to be in decline. However, a gap has emerged between the institutional organizers and the low-wage workforce they are seeking to organize.

Speaking with *Waging Nonviolence*, Hargrove disclosed that he had been working at the restaurant for just two weeks. Though many who took part in the job actions across the country were industry veterans, in Seattle, Hargrove was not unique; numerous picketers had been working at the establishments they were protesting at for less than a month. A number of these striking workers were later spotted at SEIU offices at the day's end. (When asked if their employees were taking fast-food jobs in order to agitate, SEIU officials in Seattle declined to comment.)

Further highlighting the absence of bottom-up organizing in this campaign has been SEIU's tight control over media surrounding the protests. During a day of strikes in New York City on April 4, an interview *Waging Nonviolence* conducted with a young Wendy's employee in Brooklyn was cut short when an SEIU staffer intervened. Reporters, along with a striker who had just decided to join the protest that morning, were informed that only participants with authorization were allowed to speak to the press. Reporters who wanted to talk with a worker were told to attend another rally later that day, when designated spokespeople would be present. Activists who had come out to support the strike in New York reported similar instances of conversations with workers interrupted by union staffers who wanted to make sure the activists were not representatives of the media.

From the get-go, SEIU organizers have been highly conscious of the campaign's public image. They've retained Purpose to provide the branding that has been the public face of the campaign. The company's CEO, Jeremy Heimans (who did not respond to requests for comment), has described Purpose's model as one of "movement entrepreneurship." Purpose was crafting the campaign's messaging well before the first walk-outs occurred last November. While the demand for $15 per hour and a union has resonated with a growing minority of fast-food employees, efforts by workers to become movement entrepreneurs themselves have hit stumbling blocks.

At a national conference involving fast-food workers and campaigners in Detroit last month, blogger and labor activist Adam Weaver reported that participants arrived to discover that plans for the August 29 strike had already been devised by SEIU in advance. The conference, he reported, was little more than a "pep rally." One worker told Weaver that participants began to speculate that "maybe this isn't our movement" but SEIU's.

The Fight for 15 strikes are part of a broader shift within the labor movement, an effort to regain relevance with innovative, media savvy strategies that highlight the worst abuses of the labor market. And there are plenty to choose from; paralleling the decline of unions in recent decades, earnings for U.S. workers have gradually declined as well. With the federal minimum wage worth $2 less than it was in 1968, and nearly one third what it would be had it kept pace with productivity, low-wage workers have been the hardest hit by the decline of organized labor as a whole.

SEIU is not the only union grasping for new strategies. The AFL-CIO, for instance, is seeking to add millions of non-union members to its books and to allow worker centers, which frequently organize immigrants in low-wage professions, into the the federation. Meanwhile, the United Food and Commercial Workers International Union is backing the Our Walmart campaign to improve pay and conditions at the mega-retailer.

Adam Weaver describes the SEIU-organized strikes as "militant lobbying" and a "march on the media"; he surmises that the union is likely seeking either an overall industry-standards agreement with the fast-food industry or to leverage the highly visible campaign for legislative measures to raise minimum wage levels. Both scenarios would fall short of the $15 an hour and a union the campaign demands, but they would be victories that could be seized upon to help strengthen future struggles. In any case, the direction of the campaign seems to be largely out the control of the striking workers themselves.

In Chicago, where a teachers' strike last autumn helped permeate a sense of class consciousness in the city, the fast-food campaign has taken a more organic turn. "We have explicit conversations about our vision of what it means to be in a union," said Trish Kahle, who is part of SEIU's campaign in Chicago. There, it has encompassed low-wage workplaces beyond just fast-food restaurants. Employees of Nike, Victoria's Secret and Whole Foods—where Kahle herself works—have joined in.

"The first strike we held, on April 4, was incredibly top-down," said Kahle, "but it gave people the courage to do it again and to start thinking about how they would do it differently. Now, we're in control. We have organizing-101 meetings. We discuss what to do when your boss is against you; we cover the history of unions in this country, which most of the people involved aren't aware of; and we organize around issues specific to individual workplaces."

Some insist that for organized labor to make a true comeback, it will have to rebuild itself from below.

"People stick around when they feel this is their campaign, their organization," said Joseph Sanchez, a staffer at the Brandworkers, a non-profit that has been organizing employees in New York City's food and retail sectors on a shoestring budget since 2007. "Having workers invested and developing themselves as leaders—that forms a community they want to be a part of and attracts new workers as well."

Commenting on the AFL-CIO's convention in Los Angeles earlier this month, labor historian Steve Early expressed skepticism at the zeal with which organized labor is incorporating the low-wage workers it has traditionally excluded. He argued that incorporating them into the federation has less to do with building union power in workplaces than it does with building lobbying power within the Democratic Party. Early noted a suspicious lack of "strategies for defending and re-energizing labor's existing members" at the convention.

In Chicago, at least, those on the Fight for 15 picket lines have included rank-and-file SEIU members in other industries. Kahle believes that they are finding common cause with the non-unionized workers who are just starting to organize. "They're thinking, 'I only make $10 an hour and I'm *in* the SEIU," she says. "The people on top at the SEIU aren't interested in organizing on the shop floor, but we are."

Like a mythical sorcerer's apprentice who conjures a force she cannot control, SEIU may be spawning a force that will rise above its managerial powers by encouraging workers to take direct action at their workplaces. As they gain a taste for their own power, employees in the fast-food industry might realize that not only are the restaurants they labor in theirs to master, but their unions are as well.

Joshua Stephens contributed reporting to this article.

1. Why are unions seeking to add members?

2. What steps are fast food workers in Chicago taking to form their own union?

"MAY DAY AND THE FUTURE OF WORKERS' INTERNATIONALISM," BY LORENZO COSTAGUTA AND STEVEN PARFITT, FROM "NOTES FROM 'WORKERS OF ALL LANDS UNITE?' CONFERENCE," FROM THE BRITISH ASSOCIATION FOR AMERICAN STUDIES: U.S. STUDIES ONLINE, MAY 1, 2015

Almost 130 years ago, on May 1, 1886, hundreds of thousands of American workers responded to the call of a defunct organisation, the Federation of Organized Trades and Labor Unions, for a general strike demanding the eight hour working day. Three days later, an unknown person threw a bomb at police during a protest in Chicago's Haymarket Square. Eight anarchists were accused and convicted of conspiracy for that act. Four of them were eventually hanged, two were sentenced to death and had the sentence commuted, another committed suicide in prison and the eighth was given 15 years in jail. The Haymarket martyrs, as they became known, won wide sympathy for what was often seen as a colossal miscarriage of justice and an international campaign to secure their acquittal began. When the American Federation of Labor set May 1, 1890, as the date for renewed efforts to gain the eight hour day, they gained worldwide support from socialists, anarchists and trade unionists, many of whom had defended the Haymarket martyrs, and who marched in their millions on that day in all parts of the globe.

The idea of May 1, May Day, as a day celebrating international labour solidarity was born. From then, until now, men and women across the world have tried, with varying degrees of success, to maintain that tradition and uphold the principle that underlies it. However, that task seems more difficult than ever. The American labour movement actually organised a greater proportion of workers in May 1886 than it does today, and similar reverses have taken place in most of the so-called developed world. In the rest of the world trade unions have often scored major successes—most recently, playing a major role in the downfall of the Egyptian dictator Hosni Mubarak—but they have found it difficult to match the power of the global corporations that roam the world in search of cheap labour and amenable political clients. International migration, for all its many benefits, has often complicated efforts to unite workers in different countries against the power of global capital.

These challenges were at the centre of the event "Workers of all lands unite? Working class nationalism and internationalism until 1945," a conference organized by the Department of History and the Department of American and Canadian Studies at the University of Nottingham last March 7th, 2015, with the support of the Economic History Society. After a cursory glance at the programme, with academics from universities all over Europe delivering papers concerning the period before the Second World War, one could imagine the concepts of nationalism and internationalism as once major but now extinguished forces that shaped the past of working class movements. As the keynote address delivered by Dan Gallin made clear, however, this is hardly the case. As a militant of the International Union of Food Workers and now Chair of the Global Labour Institute, Gallin has been an active member of the international workers' movement for more than fifty years. His speech, which spanned from the life and thought of the Dutch activist Edo Finmen to the recent political problems of the biggest international union of the world, the International Trade Union Confederation, was devoted to showing "how nationalism can creep into the labour movement and destroy its ideological substance." In the words of Gallin, nationalism became the enemy to fight on the road to improve workers' rights. From the First World War, to the Stalinist idea of "socialism in one country" and the 1973 creation of a neo-nationalist European Trade Unions Confederation, nationalist sentiments, argued Gallin, generally disrupted plans for inter-class, inter-ethnic and inter-racial emancipation.

The papers presented during the conference did not always support Gallin's conclusions, however. Several argued that nationalism, in specific contexts, worked as a fundamental progressive impulse against conservative and reactionary forces. Susan Garrard's (University of St. Andrews) paper, for example, discussed how Giuseppe Garibaldi, protagonist of the Italian nationalist movement, represented a model for the female Scottish working class, activating sentiments that contested the dominant framework of male British nationalism. Elsewhere, Musab Younis (University of Oxford) explained that black nationalism contributed to the advancement of African American movements in the US between 1919 and 1939. Finally, Brian Casey (University College Dublin) unveiled the role of nationalism in the construction of political consciousness amongst the lower classes in the west of Ireland in the 1870s. Other papers fell more in line with the point against nationalism made by Gallin, for example Nikos Potamianos's (Independent researcher) presentation concerning the use of "Greekness" as a way to exclude foreign workers from Athens's harbour in the 1910s, or Ivan Jelicic's (University of Trieste) paper on the difficulties of building a socialist movement in Fiume, where divisions were prominent due to the town being a crossroad of different cultures and nationalities. The other, equally impressive contributions, spanning every continent and dealing with a wide range of historical actors, fleshed out these points of view still further.

The final roundtable drew on historical experience in order to focus on the great question that faces us today: what needs to be done now? The panel, composed by Drew Allison (University of York), Dan Gallin (Global Labour Institute), Christopher Phelps (University of Nottingham) and Chris Wrigley (University of Nottingham) and chaired by the former Labor Notes editor (and member of the conference committee) Kim Moody, rapidly found an agreement on some key points. First of all, workers, now more than ever, need an international movement, one that can tackle the issues raised by a globalized system of production. Secondly, this movement must be a trade union (not a political party), because political parties are too structurally connected to national-based problematics. Thirdly, even if it is a trade union, this movement must have a political agenda, one that is not only defending the narrow interests of its members, but also addressing the problems that plague workers on an international level. On these premises, the discussion moved on well beyond the scheduled time. Indeed, debates about these questions went on well into the night, at the wine reception and the conference dinner that followed it.

As we prepare to celebrate another May Day, nearly 130 years after so many workers from all over the world first claimed that day as their own, the "Workers of All Lands Unite?" conference proved at the very least that the international labour movement still attracts fine scholarship from all parts of the globe. As for that movement today, the words of one venerable saying sum it up best—there's still life in the old dog yet.

1. Who were the Haymarket martyrs?

2. What role might nationalism play in the success or downfall of labor unions? Why?

"RESURRECTION UNIONISM—5 WAYS LABOR CAN RISE AGAIN," BY DAVID GOODNER, FROM *WAGING NONVIOLENCE*, APRIL 15, 2015

In a major blow to workers' rights and economic equality, Wisconsin governor and top-tier presidential contender Scott Walker signed a right-to-work bill into law last month, making the proud, industrial Midwest cheese state the 25th in the country to prohibit workers from signing union security agreements with employers.

The new law is almost certain to significantly weaken private-sector unions just four years after Walker succeeded in eliminating collective bargaining rights for most public sector workers in the state. The development also positions Wisconsin as a state leader in austerity, as Gov. Walker has combined his assault on organized labor with over $2 billion in tax cuts for big corporations and the super-rich, as well as a budget to cut $300 million from the University of Wisconsin education system.

The victory for Walker and his corporate backers like the Koch Brothers and ALEC is sure to encourage more union-busting efforts in states across the country. It's not hard to imagine a Republican president, maybe even Walker himself, signing a national right-to-work law in 2017 if given the opportunity.

All of this matters because, despite its flaws, organized labor is the most powerful democratic force in American history. Fewer labor unions means more income inequality, and everyday people and hardworking families are sitting ducks to the corporate agenda without the effective counter-weight of a strong labor movement.

That's why it is imperative that organized labor heed the lessons of Wisconsin, soberly analyze the outcome, and draw the right conclusions from the fight in order to inform the movement's next steps.

The most important lesson to be learned from Wisconsin is that labor's traditional electoral program is no longer effective, if it ever was. Labor and other allied groups spent tens of millions of dollars in the 2012 recall election and again in 2014 in an attempt to oust Walker, but their spending was still dwarfed by big money corporate interest groups.

Even worse was the missed opportunity cost: Labor wasted four years telling everyday Wisconsinites to elect moderate, pro-business Democrats instead of stoking the flames of a historic uprising and working to pull off a general strike. They should have used all that time and money to educate and mobilize the working class instead, to train them how to solve their own problems through organizing and collective action.

CHASING THE GOLDEN CALF DOWN A RABBIT-HOLE

Although it's difficult to accurately track election spending, particularly in the post-Citizens United era of super PACs and dark money, some labor leaders predicted ahead of the 2014 elections that unions would spend more than $300 million in nationwide races, as they did four years earlier. In 2012, labor spent $600 million on state and federal races, compared to $9.5 billion from big corporations. The Koch Brothers alone spent more than the top 10 labor unions combined in 2012.

Unions won't have to fully disclose all their 2014 election spending until October 2015 when federal reports are due. But, according to the Center for Responsive Politics, the National Education Association spent nearly $30 million in direct candidate campaign contributions in 2014. SEIU spent close to $24 million, the American Federation of Teachers spent nearly $20 million, and other unions like AFSCME, the AFL-CIO, the Laborers, and many others all spent millions more. Unions also donated millions of dollars to liberal super PACs.

These forms of election spending by labor unions don't include millions of additional dollars spent on direct member education, which is generally seen as a far more effective form of election work than campaign contributions to Democrats.

What did unions get in return for throwing all of this money at Democrats in 2014? Next to nothing, as Republicans took control of the U.S. Senate and made significant in-roads across the electoral map at all levels of government. Wisconsin's union-busting governor is now rivaling Jeb Bush in popularity in right-wing presidential circles after winning three elections in four years.

The years that Democrats have won big in elections—think 2006, 2008 and 2012—were because mass street protests changed the consciousness of millions of people and redefined what was possible. In 2006, Democrats gained control of both houses of Congress because of widespread anti-war sentiment, opposition to President George Bush's proposal to privatize Social Security, and a massive backlash against draconian immigration reform that turned out millions of people into the streets on May 1, 2006.

In 2008, President Obama won the White House largely as a result of the same sentiments and because the national economy had just crashed with a sitting Republican in office. In 2012, the Occupy Wall Street movement effectively changed the dominant public narrative away from budget deficits and toward income inequality, negating the Tea Party sweep in 2010—itself a product of opposition to corporate health insurance reform—and giving Obama a platform to win a second-term.

Mass movements dramatically changed the political landscape, while the usual game of inches played by the liberal "get out the vote" ground game in 2010 and 2014 failed to capture the public imagination and led to massive blow-outs across the country at all levels of government.

But even in the years that Democrats did well, organized labor saw virtually no pro-worker legislation passed, or even seriously debated. The Employee Free Choice Act, or card check, stalled in the Democrat-controlled U.S. Senate in 2009 and was one of the first things President Obama dropped from his bully-pulpit agenda after taking office. Labor is now in a political dogfight with their alleged White House ally on free trade.

This gloomy outlook on organized labor's electoral program is reinforced by data compiled by Kim Moody in his groundbreaking 2007 book, *U.S. Labor in Trouble and Transition*, which found that labor PACs spent between $100 and $200 million in every two-year election cycle between 1996 and 2004 and barely changed the makeup of Democrats in the House and Senate. During this same time period, no significant union priorities were passed while major setbacks such as NAFTA, welfare reform, and the repeal of the Glass-Steagall Act were all supported by many of the same Democrats labor had helped elect, including a president.

ATONEMENT, DIVESTMENT AND DIRECT ACTION

The situation post-Citizens United is even worse, and it is absolutely imperative that organized labor stop seeing their election war chests as their strongest weapon to fight big money when workers' ability to self-organize, go on strike, and shut down economic production is their only real source of power.

If organized labor is to survive and regroup from the assault it is now under, union bosses must be willing to divest from the traditional electoral platform they are used to running and use the money to reinvest in building real people power in the workplace. This money—literally hundreds of millions of dollars every year—should be diverted instead to five key areas.

1. **New Organizing**. Although some critics have argued that labor should stop spending money on new organizing campaigns and instead focus on internal organizing, the truth is organizing has brought in 1.5 million new union members even as labor unions have lost 3.5 million more. New organizing drives will lead to more union density, which will help lead to more victories at the workplace and at the polls in the long run.

2. **Internal Organizing**. Strong labor unions can only be built from the bottom-up. At its best, this is done by training dozens of rank and file workers to become union stewards and active leaders in their union, including defending their co-workers on the job and organizing them into committees capable of taking action. As relationships are built and grievance and bargaining victories are won, more workers will see the value of the union and become active members in it.

   The problem is that even labor unions that claim rhetorically to put a high priority on internal organizing often don't have the resources for it. Even the best paid organizers are often too overworked to prioritize leadership development in their bargaining units, particularly when election campaigns tend to always get in the way.

   Unions needs to start putting real money into training their own members to become activists and organizers. They could start by setting an ambitious goal to train 1.5 million new worksite leaders by the end of the year, as an initial step towards rebuilding powerful internal structures, networks, and committees to better facilitate the self-organization of the rank and file.

3. **More Worker Centers**. Worker Centers and other "alt-labor" groups are effective organizations often funded by unions to fill a niche that industrial labor is unable to handle on their own, particularly in black and

immigrant communities. Many workers in the service sector without a union turn to Workers Centers when faced with wage theft or other exploitation on the job. These organizations often lead the Fight for $15 movement in cities across the country, and this model of organizing could expand greatly with more investment from unions.

4. **Strike Schools.** Reviving the strike is key to rebuilding the labor movement. But many labor unions have all but forgotten how to take effective action on the job, up to and including going on strike. According to the U.S. Department of Labor, in 2014, there were only 11 work stoppages involving more than 1,000 workers. In 1952, there were 470. In 1974, there were 424. This is a real problem because the decline in strike activity also closely mirrors a similar drop in union density. Organized workers barely make up 10 percent of the workforce today, half of the rate in the 1930s, and down from a historic high of nearly 35 percent in 1955.

   Furthermore, as Moody shows, periods of open labor revolt generally align with large growths in union membership. Strikes work, both to win concrete victories on the job and in the political arena, but also to electrify the working class into re-imagining what's possible.

   Organized labor could start to turn these statistics around if they invested part of their election budget into "Strike School" programs to organize their bargaining units and prepare their members to go on strike. One of the best models out there was developed by SEIU 1021 in San Francisco and includes day-long presentations, videos and discussions on the theory and practice of how to prepare bargaining units to go on strike and win.

5. **Civil Disobedience.** Federal labor law has made it extremely difficult for unions to go on strike and engage in many other forms of protest, but that didn't stop labor from organizing before it was legalized in 1933, and it shouldn't stop them now either. Labor could begin training its members to take action on the job and either refuse to pay the fines and penalties that result from illegal strikes, or raid its campaign war chest for funds instead.

WE NEED BIG SOCIAL MOVEMENTS, NOT BIG MONEY

None of this is to say that elections don't matter, because they do. Elections have consequences, and the run-off primary between Rahm Emanuel and Chuy Garcia in the Chicago mayor's race is a great example of how community organizing, bold strikes and alliance-building can feed into real election work. But Emanuel's 10-point victory over Garcia on April 7 shows that the labor movement still has a long way to go before it has enough people power mobilized to take on big money and win.

The grand lesson in all this is that good social movement organizing, whether the 2011 uprising in Wisconsin or the 2012 strike by Chicago teachers, is the way forward for the labor movement. Effective election work, when it happens at all, is spurred forward more by mass movements than by mass money. Even when labor sometimes wins elections, their failure to break with the Democratic Party, who is equally beholden to big business, undermines worker victories at the polls.

At the end of the day, worker power is found on the job and in the streets, not in the campaign coffer. A fundamental strategic shift on this point is the only way forward for a crucified union movement to rise like a Phoenix from the ashes and start to truly fight back against corporate control.

1. How did the Occupy Wall Street movement affect the United States?

2. What are strike schools? Why do they matter?

CHAPTER 5

WHAT THE MEDIA SAY

Since their creation unions have been a popular topic in American media. This is partially because it is the media's job to inform the public about union activities like strikes and legal cases and partially because unions rely on media attention to gain support. Public support can help put a significant amount of pressure on companies in favor of the workers, and ultimately aid their cause. However, the contemporary media also often focuses on how labor union tactics are being successfully used for things outside of the labor market. In this chapter you will read about how students and tenants are using labor tactics to win economic justice and, in some cases, legal protections. New organizers are eager to use media attention to help inform others about the reasons and ways to begin forming their own union.

"HOW UNION STAKES IN AILING PAPERS LIKE THE *CHICAGO SUN-TIMES* MAY KEEP THEM ALIVE," BY MARICK MASTERS, FROM *THE CONVERSATION*, AUGUST 16, 2017

The recent purchase of the *Chicago Sun-Times* for a nominal US$1 by a consortium of labor-affiliated organizations and individual investors highlights the troubled state of the newspaper industry.

It also raises the question of whether union ownership can bolster the odds that this Windy City daily whose founding dates back to 1929 can survive.

Research conducted by me and others suggests that, perhaps surprisingly, giving unions a financial stake in a company can offer advantages that would not only benefit *Chicago Sun-Times* employees but the newspaper and the wider community as well.

THE STATE OF THE INDUSTRY

Regardless of who owns it, the *Chicago Sun-Times* operates in an industry wrenched by a tsunami of economic, technological and social change that has rendered the traditional business model of newspapers obsolete.

Just 20 percent of the U.S. population got its news from a print newspaper last year, compared with 27 percent in 2013. Weekday circulation for print dailies dropped to 34.7 million in 2016–the lowest in at least 77 years–down from 52.3 million a decade earlier. And advertising revenue from both print and digital dailies plunged to $18.3 billion last year from $49.4 billion in 2005.

The *Chicago Sun-Times*, which has won eight Pulitzer Prizes and was the home of legendary film critic Roger Ebert, itself offered vivid testimony of these hardships when it declared bankruptcy in 2009. This led to steep bargaining concessions by its employees after it was bought by STMG Holdings, the only bidder for the company.

For example, the paper negotiated a 15 percent cut in pay and benefits for newsroom employees who belonged to the NewsGuild union.

These realities highlight the challenges confronting the new *Chicago Sun-Times* investors, which include the Chicago Federation of Labor (CFL) union, former Chicago Alderman Edwin Eisendrath and several local labor unions. The head of the CFL is expected to be named chairman, while Eisendrath will be the chief executive.

LABOR AND THE MEDIA

While labor unions have little experience running major newspapers, they have a long history of engagement with the media, primarily to serve three explicit objectives:

1. to communicate with their members and targeted audiences regarding organizing drives and bargaining campaigns
2. to counter the often heavily business-slanted presentation of news and information through not only print but also radio and television
3. to convey broader messages for economic and social change.

The specific media through which unions have sought to realize these goals have varied. To communicate with members, unions have relied extensively on internal organs, which have morphed beyond print publications to the widespread use of social media.

However, efforts to make their voices heard beyond the rank and file by obtaining or purchasing time in the mainstream media have at times been thwarted by broadcasters, which tended to adopt a pro-business perspective.

In the 1930s and 1940s, for example, the National Association of Broadcasters (NAB) adopted a code of ethics that banned the airing of controversial issues, apart from political advertising; the code also forbade soliciting members. The code was operationalized by broadcasters to ban unions from advertising or buying time because they raised "controversial" issues like strikes and lowering the cost of living.

Unions challenged the NAB code, as administered, before the Federal Communications Commission and received some relief in the mid-1940s, but the media remained business-dominated.

In such an environment, unions resorted to establishing their own media enterprises, especially in radio. The Chicago Federation of Labor (CFL), for example, established WCFL-FM in 1926, a noncommercial radio station that promoted the voice of labor. In 1949, the United Auto Workers and the International Ladies Garment Workers Union established radio stations in Detroit, Cleveland, Chattanooga, Los Angeles and New York City.

Unions have faced several major hurdles in their efforts to reach wider audiences through the direct operation of their own media businesses. A key liability is that labor simply lacks the financial wherewithal to operate in any news-related medium on a scale comparable to corporations and business moguls.

In the *Chicago Sun-Times*' case, while the acquisition involved a token price of $1, the investment consortium had to secure funding of $11.2 million to cover anticipated losses over the next three years.

Research I have conducted on union finances has shown that the aggregated assets and revenues of labor organizations pale in comparison to the financial capacity of large companies in the U.S. Many of the wealthiest people in the world, in fact, each have far more financial capacity at their disposal than all U.S. labor organizations (local, regional and national) combined.

Another major liability is the sheer decline in labor's presence in the workplace. Today, only about 6.4 percent of the private sector workforce is unionized, compared with almost 17 percent in 1983. If membership is a proxy for union support, then union-owned papers and other media have a relatively small audience to tap directly. And this audience is by no means homogeneous in economic, political or ideological outlook.

THE DIFFERENCE A UNION MAKES

While that trend is unlikely to change, the union-backed purchase of the *Chicago Sun-Times* could potentially help turn around its flagging fortunes. To understand how, it's useful to consider union ownership in other industries.

Notably, the UAW made major economic concessions in 2009 in exchange for partial ownership of General

Motors, Ford and Chrysler through Voluntary Employee Beneficial Associations.

Though union ownership of business is not common in our capitalist system, and is often viewed skeptically by labor advocates, there are widespread uses of other forms of shared capitalism, in which employees obtain a stake in the financial performance of the business. Research indicates that at least one-half of the private sector U.S. workforce is covered by some form of such capitalism, which includes profit-sharing, gain-sharing and employee stock ownership programs.

Numerous studies have concluded that these types of shared capitalism are associated with more positive employee attitudes, higher levels of productivity and better financial performance. The impact is amplified if these financial ties are combined with employee involvement, employment security and practices that invest in employees, such as training.

My research on labor-management partnerships indicates that providing employees, through their union representatives, a bigger voice in the organization and workplace results in less conflict, improved organizational performance and cost savings.

Of course, labor ownership in newspapers won't resolve all the harsh economic realities newspapers face due to the rapid technological advances that have made the news and other information instantaneously and freely available on multiple platforms.

Still, I believe the deal struck by the *Chicago Sun-Times* and its new investors provides several avenues for unions to affect the company's employment practices so as to produce individual, organizational and societal benefits.

The placement of a union official at the helm as chairman is one such good step. It should help set the tone for labor-management relations, providing workers with job security, preventing further wage and benefit concessions and promoting the kind of investment in training and talent that will help it compete in the digital world.

Furthermore, unions may use their ownership position to present perspectives on business and economic affairs that better reflect the interests of the working class. This could potentially broaden the appeal of the newspaper and have broader societal benefits by offering more diverse perspectives.

In short, the stage is set for the union investors to show what they can do. They possess advantages which should be methodically exploited. A stronger union voice arguably promotes both industrial and political democracy.

1. How can unions affect employment practices?

2. Why do unions need the media?

"UNIONS ARE NOT CAPITALISM," BY JAMES E. MILLER, FROM *MISES CANADA*, SEPTEMBER 2, 2014

Labor unions are a dying breed. According to the Pew Research Center, union membership in America "is at its lowest level since the Great Depression." In 1983, there were approximately 17.7 million union workers. Today, that number stands at 14.5 million, with every estimate showing a continued downward trajectory. Clearly, the Norma Raes of the world are going extinct.

But as Samuel Johnson quipped, one should never dismiss the triumph of hope over experience. In celebration of Labor Day, the leftie rag *New Republic* recently published an interview with labor strategist Rich Yeselson defending the role of unions in the U.S. As a labor organizer, Yeselson's bias is on full display. Instead of giving an objective view of stagnating union membership, he obfuscates to boost his own profession.

When asked if unions are dead, Yeselson rightly says "no" while pointing out that millions of Americans are still active members. Unions not only retain fairly hefty membership, but also own valuable real estate in big cities and pension funds worth billions of dollars. Despite declining membership, there is still plenty of capital left over from organized labor's heyday.

Fancy buildings and promised retirement benefits aren't enough to reverse the downward trend however. Public opinion about unions is also on the decline. Between Volkswagen plant workers voting against joining the United Auto Workers and the confectionary company Hostess declaring bankruptcy to rid itself of unionized employees, there is a growing perception of greed directed at labor organizers. There is also the uncomforting fact that state and local governments—the industry most heavily unionized in the country—are underwater on their pension obligations. Even politicians are starting to face the truth: there is less money in government coffers than was promised. New Jersey Governor Chris Christie recently toured his state telling voters that pension funds "will go bankrupt if we don't make significant changes to it." He won't be the last to break the bad news.

Yeselson plays stupid to this fiscal reality. Throughout the interview, he defends the legacy of unions with sophistry and economic inanity. Yeselson acknowledges that unions often try to "take the wage out of competition." But, he asserts, this is not a problem. With locked-in wages, "the quality of the product, innovation, etc. are the ways that companies, ideally, compete."

This is patent nonsense. Wages are an integral part of running a business. Management can't determine costs without accounting for the price of labor. Competition in wages means business can attract the best and brightest workers. An industry without workers who compete for wages is stagnant, unable to innovate to its full capacity. For someone on the side of worker well-being, Yeselson doesn't want to see business competing for employees by offering higher wages or more generous benefits.

The biggest whopper of the Yeselson interview comes when he asserts that unions are "inherently conservative institutions which historically developed parallel with the development of capitalism itself." Ezra Klein backs him up on this point by claiming "you'll find unions pretty much everywhere you'll find capitalism." This is a classic mistake of correlation with causality. Just because the labor movement accelerated with American economic power during the twentieth century doesn't mean it helped in the process. If anything, unionization inhibited the ability of the entrepreneurs to succeed. Yeselson says unions "are as much a part of capitalism as Henry Ford or Apple." That's also incorrect; Henry Ford and Steve Jobs created products for the marketplace. Unions don't produce anything for consumers. They leech off the profits of business.

Yeselson even has the gall to say that unions are inherently capitalist because they "use contracts...to link their members to the fortunes of the companies they contract with." Clearly, Yeselson needs to brush up on his common law. Contracts aren't contracts when they have the implicit use of force at their backing. Business either chooses to bargain with unions by choice or by force. The National Labor Relations Act—passed at the height of the New Deal—compels some private U.S. companies to bargain with unionized employees. Yeselson tries to say that "contracts are not unilaterally imposed at gunpoint upon terrified managers" but "are bargained between two institutions who have both common and conflicting interests." Again, why must management bargain to begin with? Why are there deliberations over wages and benefits?

With government acting as the muscle behind unions, there is no choice. Company owners must bargain or face the threat of fines or jail time. This isn't an amicable relationship. It's a thuggish shakedown. Is it any wonder why Jimmy Hoffa is such an intolerable brute?

Ayn Rand had unions pegged best when she declared their purpose has never been to empower the average worker. "Unions and trade associations," she wrote, "are not directed against employers or the public but against the best among their own members." The goal has never been about "raising the weak in any way whatever, but simply forcing the strong down to the level of the moron."

Yeselson ends his futile attempt to defend unions by bringing out the classic trope: "Unions, as the old saying goes, the folks who brought you the weekend." This is nothing but an elementary school myth. A bunch of greasy-haired petition-gatherers didn't create the weekend. Capital accumulation and rising productivity make it possible for people to take off work at the end of the week. Otherwise, the drop in commercial activity would render a business unprofitable, and thus unable to keep the lights on. This has always been the great secret behind unionist fiction.

With economic growth still staggering, the decline of union membership can't come soon enough. Freed from the demands of overpaid bargainers, innovation and productivity inevitably rise. Increasing numbers of Americans are migrating to states with less strenuous union laws. When given a choice, workers go with their money is; not where there's tough talk about bargaining rights. Labor is important; business is important; and solidarity is important. They are all no doubt conservative principles worth maintaining. But the right of every man to choose for himself takes precedence over all. You can't build without capital; just as you can't organize without sovereign will. Unions violate the spirit of voluntary association by the very fact they have government-backing. Yeselson is lying to himself if he sees forced collective bargaining as a necessary component of capitalism. And he is doing workers a great disservice by encouraging the formation of unions.

1. Do unions affect wages?

2. What are some arguments against unions?

"WILL THE FUTURE OF THE WORKING CLASS BE DETERMINED BY THE GLOBAL SOUTH?," BY ERIC DIRNBACH, FROM *WAGING NONVIOLENCE*, JANUARY 22, 2017

The prospects of the "working class" as an agent of social change has been debated for well over a century and a half. In recent years, part of this discussion involves the weakening of the labor movement in the United States and other industrialized countries. There's certainly no question that there has been union decline in many countries in the past several decades, with the United States seeing a fairly drastic fall in union density, which currently stands at 11 percent. This is related to another strand of the discussion—the loss of jobs in former union industry strongholds such as manufacturing. Furthermore, a more combative employer class makes organizing new workers difficult and has thrown the labor movement on the defensive. Meanwhile, there's another discussion in more techno-futurist circles that speculates about the "end of work," where the future post-industrial economy will require fewer jobs and workers as the production of more goods and services are increasingly automated. Thus—in the Global North—it may seem to some that there are fewer industrial jobs, and those that remain are increasingly non-union, calling into question the notions of traditional working class identity and its agency as a revolutionary force.

However, for now, stuff still needs to be made, and raw materials still need to be dug up. But this is increasingly happening in other places. The jobs lost in the Global North often don't really disappear, they may reappear in different forms in the Global South due to continuous corporate restructuring, outsourcing and foreign direct investment in developing countries. As an example, a recent report from the Economic Policy Institute estimates that over 3 million manufacturing jobs have been outsourced from the United States to China, based on the volume of manufacturing imports.

As these jobs move from north to south, worker organizing often follows. Indeed, Beverly Silver in her book *Forces of Labor: Workers' Movements and Globalization Since 1870* showed convincingly that for over a century—in several industries such as textiles and automobile assembly—as capital moved production from country to country, labor unrest soon followed. The labor turmoil may then instigate further moves by capital, spurring further labor organizing at the newer production sites. In this way capital and labor are in a perpetual dance as employers seek lower costs and newer workers revolt against the subsequent poor working conditions.

In his new book *Southern Insurgency: The Coming of the Global Working Class*, City University of New York Professor Immanuel Ness focuses on the labor movement of the Global South. He rejects the idea that the working class is shrinking—in fact, he sees growth, movement and transformation. He reminds us that the global proletariat is at its largest size in history, currently around 3 billion workers, and that the Global South has 84 percent of the industrial workers and 74 percent of the service workers. As unions have declined in the north, the major labor struggles are now being waged by southern workers, and it is there that the future of the working class may be determined.

Ness focuses on three labor case studies in India, China and South Africa in an effort to better understand how southern workers are organizing. As these cases occur in three of the BRICS countries (the designation for five of the major developing and influential economies: Brazil, Russia, India, China and South Africa), what happens in the labor movement there is of global importance. He uses these specific examples to highlight a trend toward growing worker militancy in the form of direct action and autonomous workers' organizations. This book is a clear successor to previous books edited by Ness such as *New Forms of Worker Organization: The Syndicalist and Autonomist Restoration of Class-Struggle Unionism* and Ours to Master and to *Own: Workers' Control from the Commune to the Present*, which present examples of autonomous worker organizing and worker self-management.

THE CASE STUDIES

The three case studies have a number of factors in common. They take place in major countries that over the past several decades have become integrated into the global economy within the neoliberal framework. They include organizing among migrant workers (traveling from distant rural to industrial areas) and/or contracted workers. Traditional unions were not responsive to the workers' needs, and there has been state repression against the workers organizing efforts. Ness sees three general directions these workers have taken, which include holding worker assemblies, the formation of independent unions and the pressuring of traditional unions.

Throughout the book Ness adopts a critical perspective on neoliberal "globalization" as the latest phase of northern capitalist imperialism, and he highlights concepts such as the global reserve army of labor which is used to depress wages. He is also extremely critical of mainstream unions, which are often closely tied to ruling political parties and are frequently unable to represent workers as economies have moved further toward a finance dominated, "free-trade" framework.

The case of India deals with the automobile production sector, which has grown rapidly since the implementation of neoliberal economic policies in the early 1990s. Along with this growth has been the weakening of unions and the increase in contracted labor arrangements. The focus is on the Maruti Suzuki auto company, the largest car producer in India, owned by the Japanese company

Suzuki. Ness's "New Forms" book also included a chapter on this campaign.

The labor dispute at Maruti Suzuki was part of a wave of strikes at auto plants throughout India over the past number of years. Workers had been organizing at the company for over a decade, but the latest labor dispute occurred in 2011-2012 and centered on a new modern plant that had recently opened in an industrial zone near New Delhi. About 75 percent of the workers were employed on an informal basis, earning a fraction of what the full-time workers made. A series of tumultuous events occurred involving the formation of the independent Maruti Suzuki Workers Union, with a series of strikes, lockouts and plant occupations.

The campaign culminated with the company bringing in hired thugs to attack the workers, which was a pretext for the state to conduct a mass arrest of hundreds of workers for rioting. The brutality and repression the workers were subjected to is appalling, with many being tortured. Thousands of workers were fired.

A delegation from the International Commission for Labor Rights conducted a fact-finding visit and released a highly critical report "Merchants of Menace" in 2013. The report found that the workers had consistently raised the issues of intense production speeds, lack of rest times, unfair wage structure, unpaid overtime and their precarious job status. Management responded with violations of labor law, the government failed to enforce the law consistent with International Labor Organization conventions on freedom of association and collective bargaining, and the police interfered inappropriately in an industrial dispute. The trial of 147 of the workers for the murder of a plant manager during the labor dispute is ongoing.

The case study on China focuses on the major manufacturing region of the Pearl River Delta and Guangdong Province in southeast China and particularly the large shoe manufacturer Yue Yuen. The decline of state-owned enterprises over the past few decades along with the dramatic increase of foreign investment for the production of export commodities is a familiar story, as is the mass migration of hundreds of millions of rural workers to urban manufacturing areas. This tremendous growth has produced in recent years a surge in labor disputes. The labor rights group China Labor Bulletin maps the growing wave of strikes in China.

Ness focuses on a labor dispute in 2014 at Yue Yuen, the largest shoe manufacturer in the world with 20 percent of global production. The strike was mainly over the company's underpayment for social security benefits, a serious issue for the growing numbers of older workers in the region's manufacturing plants. Over 30,000 workers shut down the company for almost two weeks in what is considered the largest strike at a private enterprise in China's history. The police attacked the workers, but the government moved soon after to recognize the legitimacy of the workers' demands and mediate a settlement.

What's particularly interesting is the relationship between the workers' activity and the official union, the All-China Federation of Trade Unions, or ACFTU. As Ness makes clear, the ACFTU, which is the only official legal union in China, has moved to enroll tens of millions of workers from private sector, foreign-owned factories. However, it maintains a distant presence on the shop floor which gives workers room to maneuver with their own direct action tactics. This helps explain the large number of labor disputes—since the ACFTU has an underdeveloped grievance processing system, the workers have to resort to their own organizing and disruption. To some extent this is tolerated by the government, as long as the disputes remain isolated at the factory level and don't grow to form an independent organization that can challenge the authority of the ACFTU or the Communist Party.

Ness sees some advantages to this kind of dual labor system, pointing out the irony that "while most labor advocates and non-governmental organizations advocate and support the formation of independent unions recognized by the state, like those in the West, all the evidence demonstrates that Chinese workers may in fact have greater power through direct action without the existence of the restrictive labor laws that inevitably accompany recognition of Western-style unions."

This dynamic of a distant ACFTU coupled with growing direct action efforts on the shop floor is fascinating. It remains to be seen how long this trend will be tolerated by the state and how the workers' movement will evolve. Indeed, the 2008 Labor Contract Law was largely in response to worker unrest and it's likely that the Chinese government will continue to react with a combination of concessions and repression. Recently, in December 2015 prominent labor rights activists were arrested in the region.

The chapter on South Africa focuses on the strategic "platinum belt" in the North West province of the country, which accounts for 80 percent of world production, and was where the wave of strikes that led to the infamous Marikana massacre in 2012 occurred—in which 34 workers were killed and dozens more injured. This tragedy led to a governmental Marikana Commission of Inquiry and has been documented by the excellent film "Miners Shot Down." Ness's "New Forms" book also has a chapter on this incident.

As background, it's important to keep in mind the country's labor politics. As apartheid was ending in the 1990s, the country's principle labor federation, the Congress of South African Trade Unions, or COSATU, formed the Tripartite Alliance with the African National Congress and the South African Communist Party. This partnership means labor has been close to the government, but always as the junior partner. Indeed, as Ness points out, labor rights and economic equality were essentially abandoned in favor of formal political rights as the country turned toward a neoliberal framework under the direction of the International Monetary Fund.

A wave of wildcat strikes throughout the mining sector started in 2009 by migrant and contract workers seeking a substantial raise. Many of these workers were rock drillers, who labored under appalling conditions for poverty wages. The principal union, the National Union of Mineworkers, only represented a small part of the mining workforce and was consistently opposed to these actions. It lost the trust of the workers in favor of a newer and more militant independent union, the Association of Mineworkers and Construction Union, or AMCU. The labor unrest included workers at mines owned by the Lonmin Company and resulted in the Marikana massacre, the largest killing of Africans by South African police since the Soweto uprising in 1976.

This wave of militancy did win the workers a significant 22 percent wage increase, and the workers have held more recent strikes that have also won more increases. According to Ness, these gains appear to have contributed to a modern turning point in the South African labor movement. The important National Union of Metalworkers of South Africa became more militant and after criticism of COSATU's policies was expelled from the federation. We'll have to see if this, as well as the growth of AMCU, presage a significant restructuring of the labor movement in the country.

THE AUTONOMOUS ORGANIZING TREND

There's both something familiar and something new in these case studies. There are, of course, countless examples throughout labor history of tough organizing campaigns with management opposition, repression, firings, arrests, beatings and occasionally murders. Workers may make some gains or be left with little to nothing. These examples indeed follow that pattern and occur in sectors and countries that appear to be on the raw edge of the global class struggle.

What's newer, however, according to Ness, is the relationship between established unions and the new workers movement. The systematic failure of mainstream unions to respond to changes in the evolving global economy and represent workers effectively has led workers to adopt more autonomous and militant forms of organizing. As mainstream unions have grown weaker and more defensive, struggling to hold onto what they have, space has opened up for workers to organize themselves in other ways, what Ness calls "operating within the interstices of existing trade union structures." We have certainly seen a version of this in the United States with the rise of worker centers, the revitalization of the syndicalist Industrial Workers of the World, and the growth of the so-called "alt-labor" movement.

Ness's main claim of a growing militant, autonomous form of worker organizing is intriguing but will need to be supported by more than a few case studies, though his previous work has documented other examples as well. He's clearly sympathetic to this trend, as are many folks on the labor-left. If it is a growing movement, it remains to be seen how mainstream unions and the state will ultimately respond. If this autonomous organizing is successful in continuing to wring concessions from employers, unions may react to the competition by becoming more aggressive in organizing and defending workers. Moreover, there will likely be the usual attempts by the state to domesticate the autonomous worker groups and bring them into the system with labor law "reforms," contracts, grievance procedures and regulations.

Furthermore this brings up a paradox regarding how these inchoate workers' organizations will change over time. If they are unlike mainstream unions in that their anarchic, direct action-oriented style is what poses a challenge to the state and capital, then can these groups maintain this form for long? Ness sees an eventual maturation process, when "the worker mobilization that is taking place both inside and outside established structures will cohere into disciplined organizations." Perhaps that's true, but then this kind of institutionalization process may turn them into something like the existing mainstream unions and the militancy may be lost. How can this be avoided? And if it can't, perhaps workers may then begin again with something new.

As history has shown, the working class will continuously develop and reinvent various ways of organizing to meet their real needs at work, and these examples of direct and militant organizing demonstrate the continuing resiliency and courage of the working class under tremendous challenges. The autonomous wing of the global labor movement is an exciting development, and it will be fascinating to see how it evolves in years to come.

1. How are worker organizations in countries like China different from traditional American unions?

2. What kind of successes have worker organizations had in other countries?

"STUDENT DEBT STRIKERS GROW IN NUMBER AND IN POWER," BY KATE ARONOFF, FROM *WAGING NONVIOLENCE*, JUNE 13, 2017

Just over a month ago, *Waging Nonviolence* reported that 15 former students of Corinthian Colleges—the beleaguered, notorious for-profit higher education system—were going on strike; not from their jobs, or from class, but from their debt. Today, there are over 100 debt strikers. Their goal is to ramp up pressure on the Department of

Education to relieve not just the debt they incurred, but all Corinthian students' loans and declare that for-profit colleges are not, in fact, too big to fail.

"We had hundreds and hundreds of requests to join the strike," said Debt Collective organizer Ann Larson. With the initial announcement, the group invited potential strikers to sign up on their website to become part of the Corinthian Collective. A team of dozens of volunteers then sorted through strike requests in a "rigorous process," informing debtors about the consequences of striking, reading over bills from their lenders and asking them to write up brief biographies and statements about why they were striking.

The Debt Collective, which the 106 strikers belong to, is a product of the Occupy offshoot Strike Debt, which has made headlines over the last several years for buying up private debt on the market for low prices and promptly absolving it. The $13 million in Corinthian students' debt that the group purchased back in February cost just $1.

The Consumer Financial Protection Bureau, or CFPB, which is suing Corinthian for $570 million in predatory lending damages, has invited the strikers to a meeting in Washington, D.C., set to take place tomorrow. The Department of Education has further granted the collective's request for a meeting on Tuesday while they are in the nation's capital.

Ann Bowers, a 54-year old striker from Fort Myers, Fla., is in Washington, D.C., today for the meeting, and has been excited to see the response last month's announcement has generated. "People are taking notice, and that's very encouraging," she said. "People are paying attention."

Beyond the CFPB, the Corinthian system has been subject to some 200 lawsuits at the state and federal level, and delisted from Nasdaq for failing to file regularly with the Securities and Exchange Commission. Perhaps most deviously, Corinthian is charged with inflating its tuition to collect more money from students, encouraging them to take out additional private loans to fill in the gaps left by federal grants. By law, for-profit colleges are only allowed to get 90 percent of their budgets from federal funds, meaning that pumping students for other loans—either through the GI Bill, third party or in-house lending—is a veritable gold mine for companies that leaves students with outrageous debt burdens.

Adding insult to injury, Larson said that 30 percent of Corinthian students come from families making less than $10,000. "The people that suffer," she added, "are the people at the very bottom of the income scale."

The Corinthian 106, as they are now known, will also use a new legal strategy in dealing with the Department of Education. Under a little-known regulation called the Defense of Repayment law, students are eligible for a full discharge on their loans and refund of money paid if the schools they attended have violated state consumer protection laws. To date, 300 people have filed Defense of Repayment forms under the Debt Collective banner, which will be turned into the Department of Education in advance of the strikers' meeting on Tuesday. The department will have 30 days to respond.

"If they delay, we will push them," said Debt Collective organizer Luke Herrine. "We will protest, we send in more applications, we will add more people to the ranks of the strikers, we will make life hard for them."

That said, even without the Defense of Repayment filings, the Department of Education has the statutory power to wipe out Corinthian students' loans, as Larson pointed out. Since its founding, the Debt Collective has called on the Department of Education to do just that. "They're supposed to regulate education," Bowers noted, "and I feel they did not do their job correctly."

The department has threatened to remove Corinthian's funding before, but instead chose to broker a controversial deal between the system and the Educational Credit Management Corporation, or ECMC, a federal debt collection contractor. Under the agreement, ECMC would buy-out half of Corinthian's campuses and all of its student loans, with the government and the company essentially handing over the keys. In turn, the campuses will remain open and ECMC will forgive $480 million of Corinthian students' debt, reducing principal loan amounts by 40 percent over "an unspecified amount of years."

Critics of the deal have raised concerns that a collection agency has no business running an educational institution. Borrowers with federal and private loans, as well, will see little benefit from the agreement, as their debt is not held by Corinthian itself, but by either the Department of Education or private lenders such as Navient, formerly known as Sallie Mae. Therefore, even if Corinthian crumbles and loses its already scant accreditation under ECMC's inexperienced management, the Department of Education and companies like Navient will continue to collect on former students' loans by any means necessary. Also worth noting is that ECMC has played a crucial role in making student debt harder to escape, lobbying extensively for more stringent definitions of "undue hardship," a factor that needs to be proven in order for loan recipients to declare bankruptcy—now virtually impossible for most student loan borrowers.

"Where was the Department of Education when Corinthian began preying on students?" striker Mallory Heiney asked in a *Washington Post* op-ed earlier this month. Heiney, who said she sold plasma to buy groceries and make interest-only payments, added, "Corinthian Colleges had the option to threaten bankruptcy, sell its campuses and wash its hands of its financial problems. But students are stuck with their debt."

1. What is the Debt Collective?

2. What union tactics are student debtors using to gain debt relief?

CHAPTER 6

WHAT ORDINARY PEOPLE SAY

Unions are made by and for the people. In this chapter you will learn about what unions mean to the average person. While union power has weakened in the United States it's not because of a lack of interest in union jobs. Workers are drawn to union jobs because they offer more stability and on average have higher wages and safer working conditions. However, some people believe that America's focus on the importance of individualism has hurt unions. Individualism focuses on the idea that people should be self-reliant and not depend on others, but unions believe when people work together they can make workplaces better for all employees. For many Americans unions are an integral part of their family's history. Women and people of color have especially benefited from the effects of unions in the form of higher wages and less discrimination. As workers are reminded of the benefits of unions, interest in forming new ones continues to grow.

"CAN A LABOR UNION SAVE THE US MAIL?," BY DAVID MORRIS, FROM *ON THE COMMONS*, MARCH 12, 2015

POSTAL WORKERS TAKE AIM AT FALSE CLAIMS THE POSTAL SERVICE MUST BE DISMANTLED

Let's begin with the bad news. The U.S. Post Office, the oldest, most respected and ubiquitous of all public institutions is fast disappearing. In recent years management has shuttered half the nation's mail processing plants and put 10 percent of all local post offices up for sale. A third of all post offices, most of them in rural areas, have had their hours slashed. Hundreds of full time, highly experienced postmasters knowledgeable about the people and the communities they serve have been dumped unceremoniously, often replaced by part timers. Ever larger portions of traditional post office operations—trucking, mail processing and mail handling—have been privatized. Close to 200,000 middle class jobs have disappeared.

Since 2012 the U.S. Postal Service (USPS) has lowered service standards three times, most recently in January when in preparation for closing an additional 82 mail processing plants it announced the end of one day delivery of local first class mail and an additional 1-2 days for all mail. Subscribers to Netflix's DVD delivery service may soon discover the cost effectiveness of a monthly subscription has been cut in half because the number of DVD's they can receive in a month has been cut in half.

We are told the Postal Service has fallen so deeply into debt (see sidebar) that it has exhausted its borrowing capacity. There's no cash left. It's been challenging to invest in capital projects. Post offices are in disrepair. Trucks are out of date.

Now for the good news. A year and a half ago, a slate of insurgents won seven of nine national offices at the American Postal Workers Union (APWU). What? Can the election of new officers in a single union, even one with over 200,000 members possibly save the post office? Certainly not if they try to do it single handedly but there's a chance, just a chance they could turn the tide if they build an effective national movement. And that's what they're trying to do.

Facts About the True Financial Condition of the USPS

And now a few words about the USPS's widely proclaimed dire financial straits, which according to both USPS management and Congressional Republicans requires drastic shrinkage and privatization.

Back in 2002, an independent examination discovered the USPS had overpaid into one of its two pension funds by $40-70 billion. The post office was not allowed to benefit from this windfall because the CBO and OMB determined that if it did the federal deficit would increase.

To prevent this from happening Congress created a new Retiree Health Benefits Fund (RHBF) in 2006 and mandated the USPS make ten payments of $5.4 billion a year into it. The payments had no actuarial basis. They were simply intended to offset the USPS surplus.

From 2003-2006 the post office boasted a cumulative net operating income of $9 billion. In 2007, the year it made the first of its mandated payments into the RHBF the USPS lost $5.1 billion. In the last quarter of 2014 the USPS posted a $1.325 billion profit. But the $50 billion so far diverted into the RHBF makes it look like a financial basket case.

As the Postal Regulation Commission Chair Ruth Goldway has accurately observed, "The Postal Service has been a kind of cash cow for the federal government for the last 40 years."

THE NEW POSTAL WORKERS' UNION STRATEGY

The APWU's new officers are unusually experienced and talented organizers. After leading the Greater Greensboro Area Local for 12 years and co-founding the Greensboro Chapter of Jobs with Justice, President Mark Dimondstein was appointed APWU's National Lead Field Organizer in 2000 in a new campaign to organize workers in privatized mail trucking and processing operations. That afforded him important experience in the rough and tumble world of the private sector where workers have the legal right to strike (post office workers can't) and corporations have the legal right to do almost anything they want to thwart union organizers. The campaign had many successes but prolonged strikes against several companies eventually exhausted the union's strike fund and its national leadership refused repeated requests by Dimondstein and others to replenish it,

Other new officers include Political Director John Marcotte who organized a local coalition that stopped the consolidation of a plant in Michigan and Executive Vice President Debby Szeredy who led her Mid-Hudson local in upstate New York to fight their plant closure. Both she and the new Clerk Craft Director Clint Burelson also participated in a hunger strike in 2012.

The activist stance of these new leaders is evident in the tactics they embrace. Dimondstein insists, "We're not afraid of the streets. We're not in the streets enough. We need to picket, march, sit-in--not leave it to lobbying or one-on-one negotiations." He pointedly praises the actions of postal workers who 55 years ago this March took their future into their own hands by defying union leaders and staging an illegal strike against low pay and benefits and poor working conditions.

The 1970 strike galvanized postal workers and stunned the nation. "So invisible were the docile, dependable men in gray until last week that no one noticed that their passions were about to explode into a historic and ominous strike," *TIME magazine* reported a week later, "The first national postal stoppage in U.S. history and the largest walkout ever against the Federal Government...the illegal strike, which started in New York City, quickly spread to surrounding areas and gradually began marching north to New England and westward across the country, hitting Akron, Buffalo, Chicago, Cleveland, Dearborn, St. Paul, Detroit, Denver and San Francisco By week's end the strike had either shut down or curtailed service in more than 30 major cities, and was still spreading."

The strike resulted in the transformation of Walmart-like jobs into middle class jobs with good benefits and working conditions. For the first time postal workers gained the right to bargain collectively. And the APWU was born from the merger of five postal unions.

The new leadership has undertaken four overlapping and mutually reinforcing organizing strategies intended to protect their members and resurrect the public mission of the post office.

1. POSTAL WORKER ACTIVISM

One strategy is internal: instilling a renewed sense of individual activism in the APWU. Dimondstein envisions a "cultural shift from a service model to an organizing model of unionism."

People are disengaged not because they don't care but because they see their union dues as a premium to an insurance company or as lawyer's fees," he maintains. "We need to retool, to retrain people to see the union as themselves. We need to encourage workers to take their grievances directly to the boss, in groups, not just file paperwork and wait for union officials to service them. We need more of a movement, a sense of connection to the larger community, which will give postal workers hope and confidence."

2. PARTNERSHIPS WITH OTHER POSTAL UNIONS

The other three strategies are external. One involves an active working partnership with the other three postal unions. (National Postal Mail Handlers, National Association of Rural Letter Carriers, National Association of Letter Carriers). "The idea that we have different fights, it's the classic divide and conquer," says Dimondstein. Six months after the APWU election, the Postal Union Alliance was born to coordinate a fight that cuts across union jurisdictions: stopping processing plant consolidations, the closure and downgrading of local post offices, and the end of direct-to-the-door delivery and Saturday mail delivery.

3. PARTNERSHIP WITH OTHER UNIONS

The second external strategy is to expand the partnership to non-postal unions. Last year when USPS management launched a project designed to create mini post offices in big box retail stores, a step toward eliminating local post offices, this new partnership became evident. USPS chose Staples as the site of its pilot project.

In April A Day of Action generated hundreds of pickets, marches and rallies in more than 50 cities across 27 states under the rallying cry, "Stop Staples: The U.S. Mail is Not for Sale."

In May Staples Vice Chairman Joe Doody nervously acknowledged that its deal with the USPS "could become a problem if more unions backed the postal workers."

In June California's Service Employees International Union 32BJ, representing 145,000 union members in 11 states and the District of Columbia, endorsed a boycott of Staples. In July the International Association of Firefighters representing more than 300,000 followed suit. AFSCME, representing 1.6 million public-sector workers, signed on as well.

Addressing the national convention of the 1.5 million member American Federation of Teachers (AFT) Dimondstein made the case for solidarity, "We too are in the public sector, we too are meeting the needs of people. We're facing some of the same problems you are—I call it divert, defund, demoralize, demonize and dismantle." On July 12th the AFT endorsed the boycott. School supplies are a key market for Staples, accounting for up to one-third of its sales.

On July 14th Staples announced it was withdrawing from the pilot project.

4. A GRAND ALLIANCE

The third external strategy is to broaden the partnership to private as well as public unions and to build "a grand alliance between the people of this country and postal workers." On February 19h, that Grand Alliance launched the same day the APWU began negotiating a new contract, the first not only for Dimondstein but also for the new Postmaster General Megan Brennan. In a highly unusual expression of solidarity APWU was joined that day by the Presidents of the AFL-CIO, National Association of Letter Carriers, Communication Workers of America, American Federation of Government Employees, AFSCME, and the Coalition of Black Trade Unionists. Some 64 civil rights, labor, community and religious organizations had signed on with the Alliance.

The contract negotiations will tackle bread and butter labor issues including ending a three-tiered structure that gives workers significantly different amounts pay for the same job and offers new hires barely a living wage. But Dimondstein promises they will also "promote a vision of a vibrant Postal Service for generations to come." That includes fighting to regain high delivery standards, halt plant closings, expand hours of service and staffing for customers and use the USPS universal infrastructure to deliver new services such as public banking to generate new revenue.

WHAT IS TO BE DONE?

With Republicans in control we cannot expect Congress to lift a finger to save the post office. But USPS's management can do a great deal to revive this hallowed American institution even without Congressional approval if only it can be persuaded to take the public interest into account.

So far the USPS Board of Governors and its previous Postmaster General have been unwilling to do so. Indeed, sometimes they seemed to go out of their way to justify an assault on their own institution. When the Postal Service was planning to close processing centers it contracted with a market research firm to survey mailers about how they would react. Its study found that mailers would curtail their volumes so much that the losses to the Postal Service could erase any savings from the plant closures. Rather than shelve its plan USPS management buried the study and had another done based on a different format and questions that arrived at a more palatable (to management) conclusion.

USPS management's approach to closing local post offices would be welcome in the Boardrooms of Sears or Walmart but is inappropriate in a public institution. Consider that according to the USPS itself the closing of several thousand post offices would save the post office a paltry $200 million out of a budget of $55 billion but the real cost to thousands of communities and millions of Americans will be far, far greater.

The *Wall Street Journal* carried an instructive story about the unquantifiable costs that result from shutting down a post office. Closing the Prairie City, South

Dakota post office saved the USPS $19,000 a year. But as Daniel Beckman, a recently widowed farmer, observed, postal clerks kept a pot of coffee brewing and posted birth and death notices. "That was the gathering place for people to come in the mornings, have a cup of coffee or a can of pop, and visit, but we don't have that no more."

The area's only major hospital and pharmacy is in Hettinger, N.D., 40 miles away and over the state line. When someone in Prairie City quickly needed medication, a pharmacist in Hettinger would rush prescriptions to the Hettinger post office, catching the mail carrier who each day delivered to the Prairie City post office. Closing the Prairie City post office eliminated that dircct route, delaying the delivery of medicine by two or three days.

Even if USPS management simply took into account the quantifiable costs to a community resulting from the loss of a post office (an analysis that by my reading it is legally required to undertake), it would close very, very few of them. The only genuine cost-benefit analysis of which I am aware was done not by the USPS but by students in an economic class at the University of Wisconsin. They identified a tiny post office the USPS would clearly mark for closure and concluded that would save the USPS about half a million dollars but cost the community, just in increased travel time and expenses, more than $700,000.

The APWU hopes to shine a spotlight on these true costs to the public in order to recruit communities across the country into a national coalition to demand that the public interest must be taken into account.

The APWU also promises to ask USPS management to introduce new services that can benefit both its customers and its balance sheet. Public banking is one service the APWU has identified. The concept has received widespread attention since a study by the postal service inspector general concluded that if the USPS captured 10 percent of the interest and fees generated by the 68 million Americans on the fringes of the banking system it could generate $8.9 billion in annual revenue to the USPS. Dimondstein believes Congress need not approve the introduction of banking services and has suggested a pilot program noting, "a third of the Zip codes in America don't have a bank."

Union-management contract negotiations usually take place far from the public eye and involve only those at the bargaining table. But in some respects this spring the APWU is negotiating on behalf of all of us. Its intention is not only to force postal management to treat its workers with respect but to respect the unique public nature of this most public of all institutions. We all would do well to join the APWU in its Grand Alliance.

1. What was the outcome of the 1970s postal strike?

2. What are some of the APWU's strategies?

"IT'S ANTI-AMERICAN TO BE ANTI-UNION," BY CHRIS TILLY, FROM *PROGRESSIVE CHARLESTOWN*, SEPTEMBER 3, 2012

It's been a tough couple of years for public sector unions. Republican governors, notably Wisconsin's Scott Walker, have promoted laws to limit government unions' bargaining rights and make it harder to recruit members. San Diego and San Jose voters opted to cut union pensions. Not to mention looming municipal bankruptcies that stand to disproportionately threaten union members. All of this against a backdrop of layoffs, cutbacks, furloughs, freezes, and the like.

For eight years, the UCLA Institute for Research on Labor and Employment has taken the opportunity of Labor Day to assess the state of labor unions nationwide. This year, we found national unionization rates at their lowest since the Great Depression. Rates in California and Los Angeles appear to be continuing the downward trend that followed the most recent recession.

Our research, along with related scholarship, explains why conservative politicians are so keen to hobble government unions, but their arguments for doing so are misplaced.

Unions are unique in their power to open the American dream to large swaths of workers and their families. Moreover, at a time when bolstering worker wages and spending power would be a big help to getting the economy back on track, production workers' hourly wage, after inflation, is seven percent lower than it was in 1973. Organized labor's critics suggest that local and state budget crises were triggered by excessive public employee pay and pensions.

There are two problems with this proposition. The first is timing: budgets plunged into deficit when the 2008 recession and its lingering aftermath dragged down tax collections while boosting social service needs. In fact there was no corresponding jump in public employee costs that explains the sudden flood of red ink. Even more damning is the fact that after taking into account worker characteristics such as education and experience, employee wages and total compensation (including benefits) are lower on average for public employees than their private counterparts.

Why, then, have conservatives so intently targeted public sector unions? Our research tells us part of the answer: If you want to weaken unions, the public sector is where most of the action is. Public employees are more than five times as likely to be unionized as private ones. And though public employees earn less than workers in comparable private sector jobs, unionized workers do earn more than non-union workers, in both public and private workplaces.

What's more, the union wage advantage is greater in places where unions claim a larger share of the workforce—like Los Angeles. So, clearly, by weakening unions, conservatives in state and local governments think they can reduce costs for themselves and for the businesses that typically are key supporters.

But there is also an important political reason for conservatives to take aim at organized labor: They are one of the few forces, other than big businesses and billionaires, that can afford large contributions—

and they're mainly bankrolling Democrats. Though the spending power is not equal—for example, business-related sources outspent unions 14 to 1 in the 2000 election cycle—unions' ability to spend big and mobilize people has been a thorn in the side of right-leaning politicians. Even in California, where Wisconsin-style restrictions on unions would be unlikely to win public support, this November's Proposition 32 is designed to bar unions from political spending while building in loopholes that would allow corporate and wealthy donors to keep funds flowing.

It's true that unions were on the decline long before this latest salvo, falling from one-third of the workforce in the 1950s to about one-ninth today. But that's not due to unpopularity. Most Americans, in fact, give unions a positive approval rating, and most non-unionized workers say they'd like to have a union (1). It's U.S. employers who have perfected the art of the anti-union campaign, in which they ratchet up the tension, one-sided arguments and flat-out intimidation to the point where most workers will vote "no union" just to end the discord. Unfortunately decades-old U.S. labor laws do little to curb such tactics.

That's where the public sector difference comes in. It's easier for employers to keep a union out than to dislodge one; private sector workplaces are "born" union-free (think of a new hotel), whereas many government establishments come into being with a union contract in place (think of a new school). Private employers' actions are largely hidden from the outside world and insulated from political pressure, whereas public employers must contend with the glare of public scrutiny and the heat of political mobilization, limiting hardball tactics.

Critics of public sector unions do get one thing right: while public employees on average earn less, those at the low end of the job scale do average more than private sector peers. But that's because unions give a bigger wage bump to those who earn less—women, young people, people of color. Economists say we've lost a decade of financial progress because of the recession. We cannot afford to let progress toward our American values, including equality, similarly retreat.

1. To whom do unions give the largest wage bump?

2. How does weakening unions reduce cost for businesses?

"TO ESCAPE TRUMP'S AMERICA, WE NEED TO BRING THE MILITANT LABOR TACTICS OF 1946 BACK TO THE FUTURE," BY LIFE LONG WOBBLY, FROM *LOVE AND RAGE MEDIA*, NOVEMBER 23, 2016

The last general strike in the US was in Oakland in 1946. That year there were 6 city-wide general strikes, plus nationwide strikes in steel, coal, and rail transport. More than 5 million workers struck in the biggest strike wave of US history. So what happened? Why haven't we ever gone out like that again? Congress amended US labor law in 1947, adding massive penalties for the very tactics that had allowed strikes to spread and be successful—and the business unions accepted the new laws. In fact, they even went beyond them by voluntarily adding "no-strike clauses" to every union contract for the last 70 years, and agreeing that when they do strike in between contracts it will only be for their own wages and working conditions, not to support anybody else or to apply pressure about things happening in the broader society. When we allowed ourselves to lose our most important weapons 70 years ago, we took the first step towards Trump's America. We're stuck in the wrong time-line—if we want to get out, we have to bring the militant labor tactics of 1946 back to the future!

The Oakland General Strike began early in the morning of December 3, 1946, when police were trying to break up a picket line of mostly female department store clerks who had been on strike since October 21 ("Back to the Future Day"). A streetcar driver saw it happening and stopped his car. This stopped all the cars behind him. All of the passengers who were no longer going to work began immediately picketing at other businesses in Oakland, calling out those workers, and shutting down the businesses. The strike spread from there. Some important points:

1. The heroes of this story are the department store clerks who maintained an effective picket for 6 weeks, shutting down the operations of the business, refusing limitations on their ability to picket, and defending their picket when the cops were trying to break it. We

need to re-learn how to organize "hard" pickets which actually disrupt commerce, and how to defend those pickets from our enemies. We also need to reject all of the limitations that courts, and the unions, will tell us we have to impose on our pickets.

2. The streetcar driver who stopped his car when he saw the cops breaking the picket deserves an honorable mention, like Peter Norman ("the white dude" at the Mexico City Olympics). He knew which side he was on, and he didn't just keep moving. He saw fellow workers under attack and he used his power as a worker to support the right side—despite the fact that the retail workers strike had no immediate tie to his own wages and working conditions. He didn't ask his union if it was OK. He didn't wait to go back to his union meeting and ask them to pass a resolution supporting the retail workers. Basically, it doesn't even matter whether he was a union member. It doesn't even matter if he abstractly thought that women should be quitting their jobs now that World War 2 was over, or if he abstractly supported Jim Crow—he supported fellow workers against the cops. Since 1947, "secondary strikes" like that have been illegal, and his union could have been attacked by the court—but the union probably would have been training him all along that he can only strike in between contracts, and definitely not for anyone else's cause. We need to reject any limitation on our ability to strike in support of fellow workers, or to strike about things beyond our own specific workplaces.

3. The passengers on his streetcar and the ones behind it also deserve credit for immediately forming mass pickets, reinforcing the retail workers' picket and also spreading throughout the city and pulling other workers out on strike. They didn't come up with this all in the moment, they learned how to do this over years of tough strikes, including the 1934 general strike in San Francisco that also shut down Oakland. Mass pickets have also been illegal since 1947, and we've lost those traditions. We urgently need to relearn them.

4. The unions didn't call the Oakland General Strike—but they sure as hell called it off, and left the retail workers alone in the cold. The general strikes that have happened in the US have almost never been called ahead of time by union. They've almost always happened by workers semi-spontaneously going on strike in solidarity with other workers, supporting the demands of the first group and adding their own. (I say "semi"-spontaneously because the working class had years of practice and preparation leading into each strike—something that's been forcibly removed from our culture over the past 70 years.) Yet by the third day of the Oakland General Strike, the local union leadership was already declaring that the strike was over and everyone except the retail workers should go back to work. As the streetcar drivers were told by their union president, "*The International Brotherhood of Teamsters is bitterly opposed to any general strike for any cause. I am therefore ordering you and all those associated with you who are members of our International Union to return to work as soon as*

> *possible ... No general strike has ever yet brought success to the labor movement."* Once the retail workers were left to keep striking alone, it was only a matter of time before they were beaten and had to give up. If we're serious about reviving strikes, we need to prepare people as much as we can for how quickly the union leadership and the Democratic Party will do everything they can to prevent strikes from the start, and to get workers back to work.

The 70th anniversary of the Oakland General Strike is coming up in three weeks, on December 3rd. As all of our movements go into overdrive, and we all start networking and holding bigger events than we're used to, we should consider holding "Spirit of '46" events across the country on December 3rd to talk about the Oakland General Strike and the relevance of their tactics for today. This is obviously coming up very soon, but it seems do-able, and if it's presented right, could pull a lot of interest. What else can we start doing to prepare for the kind of labor movement we need—the kind that is ready to stand up to the state and the capitalists? What should we think about the calls that have already started circulating for a general strike to stop Trump's inauguration?

The "Labor for Bernie" initiative showed the potential for a cross-union, bottom-up movement that fought for big goals, overcame the separation that is built into the labor movement, and directly challenged the right of the Democratic party and the labor bureaucracy to speak for union members or the working class. We've all just seen that electoral politics are inadequate to stop fascism—it's time for union members and supporters to build a similar movement that is based on supporting all labor action, rejecting all limits on strikes and pickets whether they come from the government or the unions themselves, making all pickets effective, and spreading strikes when they occur (through so-called "secondary" strikes and pickets)—as well as driving police out of the labor movement. This movement should organize in city-wide groups independently of any union structure, inviting all workers to be involved, and then those groups could network nationally. The groups should be open to any worker, union member or not, but should keep union and non-profit staff and and high officers out. Once they get going, it is important that they consider themselves to have all of the legitimacy they need to organize pickets or call strikes, whether through calling for mass workplace meetings to organize action or through supporting minority action—these groups will need to do this because the existing labor structures will put brakes on all action by citing their no-strike clauses and respect for labor law. It's important for these groups to have a name that people can identify with, like "Labor United for All", "Labor Against Fascism", or "One Big Union."

The IWW is experiencing a sudden growth spike, as most radical left groups probably are right now. In particular, the IWW's General Defense Committee, which focuses on defense of the working class and community self-defense, is seeing a lot of interest of people wanting to start new locals. The GDC has a picket training that began with the 2005 Northwest Airlines strike, when the union was trying to tell workers to keep the pickets tame and ineffective. The training focuses on the tactics needed to hold effective, disruptive pickets and to maintain them against scabs. These tactics have ended up being very useful for community self-defense. We should try to make sure that we spread this picket training to as many of these new locals as possible, and prepare as many trainers as possible. If we're going to have the labor movement we desperately need, we're going to have to re-learn how to hold effective pickets, and how to engage in community self-defense—very, very quickly.

The growth that we're seeing shows that people think we have something to offer now that electoral anti-fascism is discredited. We should double down on our efforts to recruit and to integrate these new members. We also need to prove that they are right when they think we have something to offer. We need to organize boldly, which will inspire our new members to become active and take leadership, and will also inspire hundreds and thousands of more people to join.

We absolutely need to double down on our support for Latino workers. We need to prepare to mobilize boldly against any repression that they face, and to support them when/if they take action. They've already proven through the May Day strikes of 2005 and 2006 that they know how to organize mass industrial action better than any other group of workers in this country. We also need to emphasize our Spanish-language materials and infrastructure in an effort to make our organization a useful tool for Latino workers.

Millions of union members, and workers, voted for Trump. A lot of factors went into this, including massive undercurrents of hatred and bigotry, but it also seems that there was an economic element—many white workers saw him as the only program offering anything different from decades of factory closures, social cuts, and poverty with no escape. Our best bet to win them away from fascism is if we show that we have a real program to fight for, and win, a better world. If we can't do that, we won't. (The business union leadership have already thrown themselves on the mercy of the victor and declared that they're ready to work with Trump—but it's debatable whether he'll have any use for them.) We're on the verge of being in a similar situation for organizing as radicals were during Jim Crow—and we will have to organize in the same way, focusing on the needs and defense of the most oppressed and vulnerable groups of workers and forcing bigots at work to decide whether they'll side with the boss or with their co-workers. Someone can vote based on abstract bigotry and still choose to side with their flesh-and-blood co-workers against the boss that yells at both of them every day. And if they don't, they're scabs, and we'll have to treat them as such. As CLR James and Grace Lee Boggs put it in 1958, "*if a white worker or group of white workers after reading and contributing to the paper as a whole finds that articles or letters expressing Negro aggressiveness on racial questions make the whole paper offensive to him, that means that it is he who is putting his prejudices on the race question before the interests of the class as a whole. He must be reasoned with, argued with, and if necessary fought to a finish.*"

It's good that people are already thinking in terms of how we can use our power at work to exert pressure on our lives outside of work. We're supposed to think that we only have power at the ballot box, every four years. It's just become much more obvious to a lot of people that we don't have any power there. We need to encourage workers to think about leveraging their power at work in new ways in every possible respect. As the old slogan goes, the National Guard can't dig coal with bayonets—if the government legislates against women's reproductive rights, it can only do so if healthcare workers accept it; if the government sends more police into schools, they will only find students to criminalize if the teachers have not gone on strike. We need to push as hard as we can to break through this limitation of self-confidence, where workers think that workplace action (if they even take it at all) can only be about their own conditions. Even the head of the Chicago Teachers' Union, one of the most confrontational and inspiring unions in the country, accepts cops in schools and does not challenge these limitations. When workers do break through on this—and they've got to, sometime, somewhere—we need to be ready to support them with everything we've got.

The initial discussion of a general strike points to the kind of labor movement that we've needed for a long time and we're going to desperately require now. We are entering a period where the state will bring on all ferocity against any oppositional movement. They've also made it clear that the very existence of unions is one of their targets—Reagan focused on crushing militant unions to scare the rest; the current Republican party, including Trump, want to completely abolish unions, as they basically have in Wisconsin since 2011.

A general strike will only ever happen over the ruins of labor law and workplace contractualism. As we saw in Wisconsin in 2011, the day after people began talking about general strike, the international unions came down hard saying that nobody in Wisconsin had the authority to call a general strike, since each union's contracts prohibited striking. Ironically, if the Republicans try to pass nationwide right-to-work laws or outlaw dues checkoff, the only way to stop it would be a general strike–but the union leadership is neither willing nor even capable of calling such a strike. At the end of the day, if we believe that workers can overcome capitalism–then we have to believe that they can overcome US labor law and workplace contractualism.

We will also need to be ready for minority strikes or action when and if they happen. Many workers and union members may have voted for Trump and may actually want him to take office. We still need to create a movement that encourages and supports action by any size group of workers, whether it's individual fast food workers refusing to serve cops, or groups of workers going on strike, for whatever reason, even if they aren't the entire workforce. We particularly need to support trends where workers are taking action at work over issues beyond just wages and working conditions, and to emphasize how much potential power we have if we only use it. As we all begin holding mass meetings in cities around the country and building new infrastructures, we should plan out some kind of "flying picket" infrastructure which can mobilize mass pickets in immediate defense of any minority workplace action especially.

And what about the ideas which have begun floating around about a general strike on January 20th to stop Trump's inauguration? I would say that we in the IWW should be cautiously optimistic, but should wait and see whether this catches on more broadly before we consider officially engaging with it—in the meantime, we should emphasize our efforts to build a sustained, pro-strike culture and infrastructure along the lines of what I've written above. I want to be clear, that I think it is absolutely correct to promote as much unrest as possible (including industrial unrest) to prevent the inauguration. If there is a lot of excitement around the country for a day, or a week, or a month of "no work, no school" to prevent the inauguration, that would be a fantastic development. There are some who think that the IWW can just ignore Trump because we do not take a stand on politicians—this is missing the point of what is happening in this country and would be a disastrous mistake. The biggest challenge towards any industrial action will be the union bureaucracy. The AFL-CIO is "ready to work with Trump," and would be incapable of calling for or organizing a general strike even if they wanted to. We need to build the kind of movements which can challenge the hegemony of the business unions and call for strikes over their heads. Maybe a starting point would be agitating hospitality and restaurant workers in DC to shut down all hotels and restaurants leading up to the inauguration, or agitating media workers to refuse to broadcast anything by Trump. The main point is that there won't be one general strike that saves us and then we all go back to normal—our focus has to be recreating a culture of militant, production-stopping strikes which seek to spread through secondary strikes and mass pickets, and which take aim at all injustice in society, not just workplace issues.

Nothing is a foregone conclusion, as bad as it looks right now. One day we will raise a cooperative commonwealth from the nightmare of capitalism, and one day there won't be any more presidents to inaugurate. As surprised as we all might be to have waken up on November 9 and found ourselves hurtling towards fascism, we have to remember that sometimes we will be surprised by spontaneous outpourings of solidarity that people will show as they create new movements which leave us struggling to catch up. The protests which began the night after the election are a very encouraging step in that direction, and they still have time to spread from the street to every aspect of society.

1. Should unions be allowed to go on strike in support of other unions?
2. What are some important points about the Oakland general strike?

"REASSESSING THE RELEVANCE OF LABOR UNIONS," BY MICHAEL DRIVER, FROM *MEDIUM*, MAY 25, 2017

A certain smugness smudges the face of many twenty-first century Americans when they mention labor unions, if they ever discuss them at all. You can hear it in their voice. "*Well,*" they preen as they speak, "*I suppose there was a reason for unions once upon a time, but not anymore. Maybe they did some good a long time ago, but they're not needed now.*"

Those same Americans nervously eye economic indicators for signs of instability. They worry about the value of their stock portfolios and 401ks, wondering if they will hold up until they can retire. They have even begun to express concern for artificial intelligence and automation, no matter what their field of work.

Many of these Americans would claim to be "professionals" of some sort who twitch at the thought of joining many others of their ilk who are jumping, willingly or not, into the untethered world of freelancing. Many are also "white collar" workers whose once envied jobs that secured middle class status have declined in both prestige and pay, reducing them to precarious circumstances and an uncertain future.

That so many naysayers remain solidly opposed to labor unions should be surprising, given that many have parents or grandparents whose union membership was a ticket to a better life for their families. Besides the passage of time, what happened? There's not one answer but a complex weave of attitudes that all of us should hasten to understand, most of all the union doubters.

IN LIGHT OF HISTORY

Let's start with the worker generation gap that provided sufficient time for seepage of ignorance and conceit reinforcing the allegation of irrelevance. A little comfort and security went a long way toward creating distance and fertile ground for excuses and preferred, if false, explanations. In other words, a swamp formed that filled with received wisdom and assumptions that what worked in the past was no longer relevant. A feeling of superiority developed along with shock that anyone lately could identify reasons that unions remain viable.

A lot happened for sure. Long ago, there was agriculture and artisanship, then agriculture and industry, with technology altering the nature of work every step of the way. *Then there was just industry, agriculture having been shorn of employment. Right? Mechanization absorbed almost all the agricultural jobs didn't it?* In the minds of many people, it did, but thousands of agricultural workers, many of them migrants and many of them immigrants, would lift their voices in the fields to disagree. It's just that they're out of sight of most consumers and do not fit the popular imagination of what farmers do or what they look like. So, agriculture is still there, along with its employees, but in the experience and minds of most Americans, these workers ceased to be a factor.

What about industry? It a little bit plays on the conscience of some that technology eliminated many manufacturing jobs with many more disappearing off shore or over the border. *Globalization. It can't be helped. It's just the way things are now. Besides, there are still some good manufacturing jobs in the United States. Just look at how built-up the automotive industry has become in the South* (where unions are almost as scarce as Chateau Margaux in a redneck bar and wages are as low as conservative conspiracies can force them).

Finally, for displaced manufacturing workers, there is a place to land—the service industry. It's a little more disturbing to the conscience of a few more people that new jobs that manage to surface in recent years don't measure up to the past in terms of skills, wages or prospects for the future. *So, permanently laid off workers accustomed to the $26 an hour average manufacturing wage, you'll be welcomed at McDonalds or Walmart where you can* *put on a smiley face for $10 an hour or even seven-twenty-five where, sakes alive, it's a living. Right?* You know better and so does everyone else whether or not they are willing to admit it.

Willingness to see the present realistically is a large part of the problem. There is ample historical basis for this blindness. Think back to what you were taught in school. Teachers lauded American individualism at every turn. Part of it was the great man thesis writ large in a landscape of giants like George Washington, Thomas Jefferson, Abraham Lincoln and Booker T. Washington. Part of it was personal assertiveness. Teachers loved Henry David Thoreau, the ultimate individualist who built a cabin in the woods where he could commune alone with nature. All very admirable. Truly. But they didn't mention that he ventured back to the village and mooched off his parents, because, you know, food.

The takeaway from all of this is vast personal ability and self-reliance, a regard and commitment to individualism that became the national religion. Think Carnegie, Ford, Edison and Gates. If they can do it, everybody should be able to. Just look at Horatio Alger and the thousands upon thousands of examples he presumably spawned.

Americans were left with the impression that to rely on someone else was akin to religious heresy. It was completely unAmerican. To make headway, labor unions stressed the brotherhood and sisterhood of workers, a familial bond almost lost in modern culture and one that all of us desperately need to revive. Instead of flying in the face of individualism as management claims, the cooperation espoused by unions that encouraged the development of common interests served to buttress a realistic type of individualism valuing justice and economic well-being in support of families.

Management, falling back on historic interpretation of old-time individualism, proclaimed that "right-to-work" laws are its natural consequence. It was a stroke of semantic genius. Generations of Americans were misled into believing that "right-to-work" law was what it said. *What could be more American than good old self-reliant work?* In the short-term, the result was work under contracts negotiated by unions that cannot require that workers benefiting from those contracts belong to the union. It amounts to a perversion of individualism enforced by fiat. Stretch that further and you wind up with subsequent management claims that no fees whatever should be recoverable from benefited workers. No fees, no union.

The laudable concept of individualism was badly distorted for the purpose of deceit. But it worked. Today, less than seven percent of the non-governmental workforce is unionized, down from a high of one third in the 1950s. Many workers, especially union members, advanced to better lives in a solid middle class. Much has happened since then, including the erosion of middle class living standards and a brake on social mobility.

Unfortunately, many younger people, having progressed in various professional pursuits, not only fail to empathize with the plight of workers but do not want to identify with unions in any way. More is the shame and the pity for them. It should be apparent by this point that morally rendered history justifies the hard fought gains won by workers acting collectively. It behooves those who cannot appreciate the value of past sacrifice to reevaluate the origins of their comfort and see the urgency to reconnect actions with consequences. American workers stand in need today.

FACTS OF THE CURRENT PLIGHT

Lest there be any doubt concerning the current economic status of workers and how their circumstances frayed as union participation diminished, let's review a few quick facts:

- The minimum wage has not kept pace with the times. If it had increased at the rate of worker productivity, the current minimum wage would be over $21 an hour instead of the measly seven bucks and a quarter today.
- Political preference for less government at all levels means that there are fewer government inspectors and regulators to enforce laws that were intended to benefit workers. Less government means less help, forming twin pincers against the best interests of workers.
- Many localities served up their tax base as a sacrifice to attract new industry. What do they do now?
- Non-unionized manufacturing plants have more and worse accidents than facilities where the workforce has union representation.
- Lack of union representation means less safety and other types of valuable, sometimes life-saving, job training.
- Workers' compensation programs are under siege. Reduced standards for employer participation and insufficient compensation endanger workers and their families. In addition, a management group has been formed to encourage alteration of state laws that will further erode worker protections.

- Politicians in at least two states have proposed weakening child labor laws.
- Lack of adequate healthcare means a workforce subject to illness with consequent loss of income.
- Families torn by economic strife are less able to cope in society and suffer greater poverty, more health problems, lower life expectancy and higher suicide rates.
- Issues related to family preservation and healthcare for women receive inadequate attention with consequently high child poverty rates and loss of income for women.
- Unions help prevent gender wage discrimination.
- Unionized workplaces experience less racial discrimination and restrain capricious management as well as bigoted co-workers while encouraging harmonious communities.
- Punitive scheduling practices, scarcity of full-time positions, lack of affordable child care and failure to achieve a full employment economy bear heavily on the lives of non-unionized workers.
- Wage theft is low in businesses where workers have union representation but rampant in industries where employers are free of scrutiny. Laws without the diligent oversight provided by unions result in low enforcement and loss of badly needed wages.
- Low wage, non-unionized employees whose working conditions and compensation were hostage to unsympathetic politicians and the remorseless greed of large corporations have been able to derive some benefit from leadership provided by labor unions but remain poorly treated by the businesses that employ them outside the terms of union contracts.

- Ridiculous non-compete agreements forced upon workers, often unsuspectingly, make it difficult for them to change jobs.∞
- The push by states to pass "right-to-work" laws continues. A majority of states now have them on the books. The financial capability of unions have been greatly curtailed with consequent harm to workers.
- Government employee unions are under record siege, not only from states, but also from federal determination to break them, sometimes through budget cuts and layoffs.

Where unions were uprooted, problems returned. Where they were blocked, a thicket of difficulties overwhelms the economic and cultural landscape. The average union worker earns $10,000 more per year than the average non-unionized worker. That is enough to make significant difference in the lives of workers and their families. In the lowest paid jobs, a boost from $10 to $15 an hour would make a critically important improvement in the quality of life. These workers are dealing not merely with bread and butter issues, but with survival.

With so many severe problems to be conquered, it should be obvious that labor unions can make a huge difference today. Even partial remedy would make a significant difference in the lives of workers but securing representation will be extremely difficult. Everyday, management focuses on ways to defeat, restrain and block unions. Forging a path ahead will be difficult and painful but failure would be catastrophic.

These are some of the current issues in a hard-to-crack nutshell. For those who still cannot understand the importance of labor unions or who think that, at best, they are for some other group of workers in some other industry, think again. Think about contemporary issues that are tightening like a noose for more and more workers. And think about the future—your own future.

FUTURE EMPLOYMENT AND UPDATED LABOR UNIONS

Work and workplaces emerging in the twenty-first century differ significantly from what evolved previously. The pace of change is now relentless and quickening, so much so that the head-spinning reordering of our work lives makes it difficult to see the big picture and make plans for the future.

Management would have everyone believe things are better. When pressed, they cite the fact that there are few strikes these days, an indication, they claim, of worker satisfaction. But they would prefer not to dwell on issues that are so twentieth century.

Management wants us to believe the transition from unionized workforces to nonunion workplaces is beneficial and that much of the work today is done in the quiet atmosphere of benign circumstances that characterize modern facilities. These tropes are intended to undermine discontent and deflect attention from problems.

Management today doesn't employ thugs to enforce their will. Instead, they play upon the minds and sentiments of workers, taking advantage of existing predisposition of union distrust to keep pay low and working conditions glossy but barely tolerable. When employees do not want to identify with unionized workers, they play into the hands of management that wants everyone to ignore the fact of better wages and working conditions in a union environment.

Similar perversity is used to attack unionized public employees. Teachers, for example, are demeaned while being paid poorly, their jobs threatened by discredited privatization schemes that pay even less than public schools. It is, of course, of no importance to management whose children attend elite private institutions. And they look askance at all public employment. It's beneath them and they want everyone to think of unions the same way.

Not soon enough, management may doom themselves with their own cleverness, inadvertently inflating doubt about union relevance in the modern workplace to explosive proportions. Why explosive? Because the truth emerging in contemporary work and workplaces is so shocking, no management lie can contain it in the future.

The trend toward a "gig economy" encapsulates many aspects of emergent change, shifting the burden of all responsibilities onto the shoulders of individuals where trouble can fester without concerning management. Businesses never wanted to deal with healthcare issues and all the other problems of employees. Unattached and devoid of representation, freelancers are on their own, come what may.

Freelancing is a hodgepodge of talent and hyperbole vying for the attention of resources and wealth concentrated in a few large companies and many struggling businesses that need help but lack consistent means of paying for it. Sometimes placed by agencies, freelancers work entirely apart or alongside direct employees, ultimately receding into stress and a precarious future without essential benefits.

Management is as eager as a few celebrity freelancers to tout the advantages of working where and when you please. But wherever, whenever work is still work. Lush surroundings, such as the indoor forest being cultivated by Amazon, is wonderful for the few who experience it, but what about productivity demands that are draconian and HR policies that reflect nineteenth century sensibilities? We don't hear much about that but workers trapped in those situations feel the pain continuously.

Ever higher education is often said to be the answer. But with student debt already swamping many, it's hard to see how the future can expand when the past has a priority call. Privatization of public schools teaches the wrong lesson from the outset. Workers should not expect always to be paying The Man, especially when, in return, the ticket being purchased drops them off in Nowhere.

Ideals once counted for something and respect was accorded simply for being. Not anymore. Those willing to claw their way up, soon find the muck virtually impenetrable. Who knew that the study of ethics should also include instruction on whistleblowing? Organizations regularly sidetrack the careers of employees who fail to carry their assigned freight of wrongdoing. Spectacular examples such as Wells Fargo may seem like system wide failures but they actually serve larger interests. By denouncing culprits caught red-handed, other businesses claim piety while using the distraction to advance their own nefarious schemes and entrench them for the future.

Workers unwilling to admit the meaning of their experience are apt to be more compliant for the next malfeasance thrust upon them. This perverse method of separating the righteous from the unrighteous is joining technology to create two different employment paths for the future. Along one path will tread those who are incapable of utilizing technology and those who are unwilling to cede their moral underpinnings. The other path, the more remunerative one, will be populated by tech savvy go-getters and amoral, avaricious exploiters. Journalism comes to mind.

We already see how one important industry is handling this fork in the future. Only those fluent in technology now have a place in journalism. Of course, journalism subdivides into high and low roads, but, of the few journalists left standing, all are digitally fluent and all eat at least one decent meal a day. The same cannot be said of all university professors.

In one of the conspicuously important fields where technical facility is of marginal value compared with sheer intellect, many adjunct professors are shunted into second and third low wage jobs merely to feed themselves for the privilege of sharing their love of knowledge. While no specific villain can be fingered, many universities are suspiciously mired in money even as some faculty members are penurious.

Regardless of educational attainment, many workers are finding themselves channeled onto the low wage track to Nowhere. Management is doing its best to move as many workers as possible onto that track. They know, and many workers are beginning to see, that automation will assist management in their goal. Positions will be cut, wages slashed and lives crushed.

Management, meanwhile, proudly points to *exciting new opportunities in startups and developing industries.* They mean jobs in customer service—*no sweatshop there—only workers with computers* who can't disengage from their screens long enough to see the big picture of endless exploitation. Simultaneously, old style jobs are being dumbed down so that less experienced, less educated, lower wage workers can perform the tasks until robots finally take over.

Yes, revolutionary new products are being created, and yes, there will be some good jobs for a few. Emphasis few. And fewer. But the message here is that jobs are mostly low wage, both for young workers in new businesses, and for older workers in companies being revamped with technology.

Freelancers need to recognize that they are left to fit in wherever a temporary need exists and almost all the temp slots are low wage, regardless of the skills demanded. The glamour of being your own boss is rapidly declining into marathon sessions before your computer, sitting there in your underwear hour after hour for what (it's unregulated, after all) turns out to be subminimum wage.

THE FUTURE AND THE ESSENCE OF RELEVANCE

If you can't see the possibilities here for yourself and your children, the future will run over you like a self-driving truck. If you continue to deny that labor unions have an important role to play in support of future workers, it's because you've been brainwashed by the irrelevance lie. You're not alone. Management has been pushing cultural brainwashing for decades. But workers are beginning to wake up. Endless issues need to be faced that are better addressed collectively.

Nothing will happen, however, until perceptions and expectations change. All employees, including managers, must realize that everyone who works is a worker with common interests at variance from those of the mega rich. Workers in offices, laboratories, computer centers and elsewhere need to stop thinking that what they do is not the work done by union members.

Labor unions need to comprehend the challenges faced by workers outside the realm of their historic representation including high-tech industries and offices of all types. They need to seek small units of workers as well as large numbers. They need to represent professionals and service workers of every sort. They need to promote flexibility in proposals to employers, seeking sometimes unorthodox means of serving workers. Unions and freelancers also need to embrace each other and work together to confront management. The work environment is changing rapidly and unions must hasten to change with it.

Voters need to make it clear to elected officials that public policies must benefit workers. No one who works is looking for a handout; they are willing to work for everything they receive. But the concept of fairness upon which pay for work is based must be preserved for the economic system to function as advertised.

The traditional expectation in the United States—all too often a mythical expectation—is that government will secure justice for everyone equally, ensuring fairness of treatment for all parties, even when one has an advantage. The mid-twentieth century idea of big business battling big labor has long since ceased to function as labor suffered defeat after defeat under ferocious assault by management cunningly allied with public officials in debt to business. Citizens need to demand that government reassert its active role as guarantor of justice.

There is no justice in wages that fail to cover essentials of life. An employer that operates in disregard of basic human rights is unfit to dictate the terms of work. Workers and labor unions will have ample opportunities to demonstrate their resolve in the struggle ahead. Relevance must be reestablished in the minds of workers as well as in the deeds of labor unions.

Consider the myriad issues and how they apply in each workplace. Consider also the prospect that a collective response by workers is more effective than individuals tilting at unified, demanding, defiant and belligerent management. Then ask: Are the benefits of a labor union really irrelevant today and for the future?

1. How does a focus on individualism harm workers?

2. What is the gig economy? How does it harm workers?

"A SMALL THOUGHT ON LIBRARY AND TECH UNIONS IN LIGHT OF A LOCKOUT," BY GALEN CHARLTON, FROM *META INTERCHANGE*, SEPTEMBER 8, 2016

I've never been a member of a union. Computer programmers—and IT workers in general—in the U.S. are mostly unorganized. Not only that, they tend to resist unions, even though banding together would be a good idea.

It's not necessarily a matter of pay, at least not at the moment: many IT workers have decent to excellent salaries. Of course not all do, and there are an increasing number of IT job categories that are becoming commoditized. Working conditions at a lot of IT shops are another matter: the very long hours that many programmers and sysadmins work are not healthy, but it can be very hard to be first person in the office to leave at a reasonable quitting time day.

There are other reasons to be part of a union as an IT worker. Consider one of the points in the ACM code of ethics: "Respect the privacy of others." Do you have a qualm about writing a web tracker? It can be hard to push back all by yourself against a management imperative to do so. A union can provide power and cover: what you can't resist singly, a union might help forestall.

The various library software firms I've worked for have not been exceptions: no unions. At the moment, I'm also distinctly on the management side of the table.

Assuming good health, I can reasonably expect to spend another few decades working, and may well switch from management to labor and back again—IT work is squishy like that. Either way, I'll benefit from the work—and blood, and lives—of union workers and organizers past and future. (Hello, upcoming weekend! You are literally the least of the good things that unions have given me!)

I may well find myself (or more likely, people representing me) bargaining hard with or against a union. And that's fine.

However, if I find myself sitting, figuratively or literally, on the management side of a negotiation table, I hope that I never lose sight of this: **the union has a right to exist.**

Unfortunately, the U.S. has a long history of management and owners rejecting that premise, and doing their level best to break unions or prevent them from forming.

The Long Island University Faculty Federation, which represents the full time and adjunct faculty at the Brooklyn campus of LIU, holds a distinction: it was the first union to negotiate a collective bargaining agreement for faculty at a private university in the U.S.

Forty-four years later, the administration of LIU Brooklyn seems determined to break LIUFF, and have locked out the faculty. Worse, LIU has elected not to continue the health insurance of the LIUFF members. I have only one word for that tactic: it is an obscenity.

As an aside, this came to my attention last week largely because I follow LIU librarian and LIUFF secretary Emily Drabinski on Twitter. If you want to know what's going on with the lockout, follow her blog and Twitter account as well as the #LIUlockout hashtag.

I don't pretend that I have a full command of all of the issues under discussion between the university and the union, but I've read enough to be rather dubious that the university is presently acting in good faith. There's plenty of precedent for university faculty unions to work without contracts while negotiations continue; LIU could do the same.

Remember, the union has a right to exist. Applies to LIUFF, to libraries, and hopefully in time, to more IT shops.

If you agree with me that lockouts are wrong, please consider joining me in donating to the solidarity fund for the benefit of LIUFF members run the by American Federation of Teachers.

1. How could unionization help information technology [IT] workers?

2. How could unions protect us from ethical issues in technology?

"LABOR DAY 2015," BY CAITLIN AH, FROM *ESSENTIALLY A NERD*, SEPTEMBER 7, 2015

Wishing someone a happy Labor Day has always seemed a bit strange to me. It's a day to celebrate organized labor, to acknowledge those who fought and died for things too many take for granted today: an eight-hour workday, a five-day work week, *a weekend*, a day off, an age limit. It wasn't so long ago, here in the U.S., that little kids worked factories, or were newsies; it wasn't so long ago that workers had no guarantee of breaks or time off. (Per Illinois state law, workers are supposed to get two 15-minute breaks and a 20-minute lunch break per 7-hour day. It isn't much, but it's something.)

Despite coming, on my mother's side, from an old and dignified family that probably never dipped its toes in anything connected to labor, I have the movement in my blood–from a paternal great-great-grandfather (Karl, natch) forced out of his homeland for his communism and unionizing to a mother who has belonged to a musician's union for more than fifty years, to a grandfather who encouraged his employees to unionize and a father who was part of an ultimately futile attempt to unionize labs, to me, who spent four years active in a teachers' union, including several as a member of its Grievance Committee, the quest for workers' rights has been a part of my life as long as I can remember.

The Dropkick Murphys demand that their listeners think about What Side You're On. There was really never any question for me–I never crossed a picket line, I went occasionally with my mother to stand in solidarity, I chose a graduate school in part because its TAs were unionized, and immediately became active with my union. My work wasn't always easy: though I primarily served in a back-room capacity, much more conducive to my own issues with shyness, it was often heartbreaking work. One is endlessly reminded of how far we have yet to go, even as we know how far we have come. And, of course, one knows that one could not move towards that greater good without one's companions: when we all stand together, we are considerably harder to defeat. For that matter, I worked with some of the most wonderful people I have ever met while a member of the grievance committee. We all gave of our time–and it was often *a lot* of time–to strive for the best for our membership. It was truly an exercise in striving for the greater, or the collective, good.

Now, of course, the U.S. is one of the only countries around to have its Labor celebration at the end of summer, rather than on May 1, in remembrance of the Martyrs of Haymarket. Even worse, as this article from *Jacobin* notes, Labor Day was signed into being after Grover Cleveland broke the great Pullman Strike–a tarnished day, a day of infamy more than celebration. (PBS posits that Cleveland was hoping to make workers forget about his strike-breaking. It didn't work, and he lost the election.) If anything, the ugly roots make it more essential to remember that Labor Day *should* be both a celebration of the worker and a time to remember, and to plan. The struggle is a long way from over: across the country, anti-union and anti-worker legislation has been passed, and the flames of anti-worker sentiment have been fanned.

My union experience was perhaps a bit different from many: a teachers' union, ours represented teaching assistants and graduate assistants at an R1 in the cornfields. Cornfields or no, our struggles were consistent with workers' struggles everywhere, and being a member of the grievance committee required not just time but also a tremendous emotional investment. It was taxing enough, emotionally, that I had to step away–yet I know that we did good work, and I know that others continue that work now, though so many of us who served together have graduated and moved elsewhere. And, as I know from my work in the union generally, and from my service on the grievance committee specifically, many of today's unions stand for equality.

While in many ways this began even earlier, the 1968 Memphis Sanitation Workers' Strike, supported by Martin Luther King himself, marks a very decided turn towards workers' rights and civil rights combined. Today, women and people of color are much more likely to receive equal pay for equal work when they are unionized.[1] Today, the fight for a $15-minimum wage continues. It's a fight led largely by women and people of color, an organizing swell that may have been, as the Guardian tells us, the largest work action of its kind by low-wage workers in U.S. history. It's inspiring and heartbreaking–and it's worth pointing out that someone probably can't live on 15 bucks an hour, either, although they'll come a lot closer to having a living wage at $15 than at, oh, $7 an hour.

Illinois' statewide minimum wage is currently $8.25, but a bill has been passed to raise it by 2019 to $11–still pretty low, if one lives in the Chicago area. And Chicago's minimum wage has recently risen to $10...still a long shot from a living wage for someone in Chicago. For those wondering, it costs a fair bit to live in Chicago–though, as one of my uncles often says, it costs a fair bit to live anywhere.[2] (Since he lives like an ascetic monk, he's not exactly talking about paying for fripperies.) Unions fight for a living wage–we fought for a living wage, trying to bring our union's base pay up to living wage level. (Spoiler alert: we've yet to win such a thing, though we have won such concessions as modest insurance coverage, the right to spaces for breastfeeding mothers, and tuition waivers–which are always under attack.)

I was an officer (yes! me, who prefers to blend into the background!) during a contract negotiation cycle, and my fellows and I sat around many a pizza and coffee-strewn table, debating for hours. Someone once told us that *nobody* had meetings as long as we did. I'm still not sure if that is a mark of honor or simply of insanity, but there we were, and there our successors will be again, soon enough. It was terrifying: if we struck, could we win? How long could we hold out? Some of us would have held out on principle, yet principle does not pay the rent or put food on the table, and many of us (me included) do not come from families with money. But for the most part we did not need to worry about being killed–something those who paved the way for us had. Striking workers in Milwaukee were massacred in the 1886 Bay View Massacre as they took a stand for an eight-hour day.[3] Frank Little was lynched for his work. Largely immigrant strikers in Pennsylvania were massacred by a sheriff's posse in what is today known as the Lattimer Massacre. And tragedies such as the Triangle Shirtwaist Factory

Fire, in which nearly 150 workers, mostly women, were killed, led to increased organizing–and, in the case of the Triangle Factory Fire, to an upswing in women's involvement, spurred by reformers including the activist Rose Schneiderman.[4]

Much of what was won by the suffering, imprisonment, and deaths of those who came before us is being chipped away, sometimes overtly, sometimes more covertly. A full-time week is supposedly around 40 hours, yet a Gallop poll from 2014 shows what many of us have long known: it's more than 40 (they figure the average is around 47 hours). And, as this BBC Labor Day article discusses, many Americans are afraid to take their vacation days, lest they be let go. (My family has not taken a vacation in around a decade, thanks at least in part to the recession and its job losses and lowered pay.)

When I became active in my own union, I found a space where my voice could, and would, be heard; where I could, occasionally, stand out, something possible for me only because I knew I had so many brilliant, dedicated people at my back. (I like to think Great-Great-Granddaddy Karl would have approved, but I don't actually know a thing about him other than his rumored communism and his legendary labor activism, so who knows?) Despite the old, tired, and untrue stereotype of unions as a bastion of machismo and masculinity, mine was heavily female, including our co-presidents, one of whom was also our lead negotiator. (She was brilliant.) We were hardly the first women to be active in organizing, however. In 2014, the Zinn Project released a list of Women in Labor History, ranging from the quiet historical (Mother Jones, Lucy Parsons, and Hattie Canty, among many others) to the contemporary (including Ai-Jen Poo, Dolores Huerta, and May Chen), though there are several (including the president of the Chicago Teachers' Union, Karen Lewis) missing from their list.

Without women like Lucy Parsons and Emma Goldman and Mother Jones and Hattie Chanty, we might not have been taken seriously as a union, run not only by PhDs and Master's candidates but also largely by women. We have certainly built upon their gains, just as another union–or maybe even our own, in years to come–will build off ours.[5] I built on a more intimate platform: that of my mother's years in a union, and of my father's failed attempts, and of my great-great-grandfather Karl, who arrived in this land an exile. I built it around the towns from which I come: my hometown, Chicago, with its history of unions and of manufacturing; the small, dying Wisconsin town that has been home to my father's family for well over a century; the small Wisconsin manufacturing city to which my mother moved, after her family left the East (that town was also a union town). I also built around the faith in which I was raised–as far as I'm concerned, it's testimonies (peace, equality, integrity, community, simplicity–totally not my fave–and stewardship) are completely compatible with a social justice driven union. And I worked to help build a sturdier foundation, including rulings from the Illinois

Labor Board, for those who would come after me: for my brothers, S and E, and who may one day attend the same R1 institution; for my friends still there; for the grad students to come; for other unions, other workers, in Illinois and, I would like to think, elsewhere. It's one of the incredible things about being organized: alone we are so little, both figuratively and literally, but when we stand together, we are so, so much more.

Solidarity, on this Labor Day!

1. Should workers cross picket lines?
2. Why did women become more organized after the Triangle Factory Fire?

CONCLUSION

It's easy to take the successes of the labor movement for granted. Many people forget that along with the forty-hour workweek and paid vacations we can also thank unions for child labor laws, minimum wage, pensions, the ending of sweatshops, and many other things. Unions aren't just beneficial for union members. They set the bar for what is considered acceptable working conditions and wages.

Unions have shrunk in America, largely due to "Right to Work" laws. The organizations may be smaller, but leaders like Ai-jen Poo, who founded the Domestic Workers United (DWU) haven't given up defending workers rights. In 2010, the union helped convince New York to pass the Domestic Workers Bill of Rights. The law guaranteed labor protection for people who work "inside the home" like child care workers and domestic servants.

Academics and activists alike see a connection between stagnating wages and the weakening of union power. While the government and current justice system may not be union-friendly, workers continue to organize. As the gig economy continues to grow the nature of work in America will also change, the same way it did during the industrial revolution. Workers will face new challenges and require new safety measures. While unions will need to adjust to these new challenges, tactics like strikes and collective bargaining remain powerful tools for workers. As the Corinthian students and the Fight for $15 group have shown, when people are united in their struggle for justice they can win. There is power and political clout in organizing together, which is what unions do best.

BIBLIOGRAPHY

American Federation of Labor v. American Sash & Door Company. US Supreme Court, January 3, 1948.

Aronoff, Kate. "Student Debt Strikers Grow in Number and in Power." *Waging Nonviolence*, March 30, 2015. https://wagingnonviolence.org/2015/03/student-debt-strikers-grow-number-power.

Baird, Charles W. "The Myth of Compulsory Union Membership." Foundation for Economic Education, March 1, 1998. https://fee.org/articles/the-myth-of-compulsory-union-membership.

Caitlin AH. "Labor Day 2015." *Essentially a Nerd*, October 7, 2015. https://essentiallyanerd.wordpress.com/2017/09/05/labor-day-2017-the-camaraderie-of-a-union.

Charlton, Galen. "A Small Thought on Library and Tech Unions in Light of a Lockout." *Meta Interchange*, September 8, 2016. https://galencharlton.com/blog/2016/09/a-small-thought-on-library-and-tech-unions-in-light-of-a-lockout.

"Collective Bargaining." NY Constitution.org. Retrieved June 4, 2018. http://nyconstitution.org/issue/Collective-Bargaining.

Costaguta, Lorenzo, and Steven Parfitt. "Notes from 'Workers of All Lands Unite?' Conference, 7th March 2015." British Association for the American Studies, May 1, 2015. http://www.baas.ac.uk/usso/may-day-and-the-future-of-workers-internationalism.

Cunningham-Cook, Matthew. "Unions Lose Their Gamble on Beltway Politics." *Waging Nonviolence*, February 10, 2013. https://wagingnonviolence.org/feature/unions-lose-their-gamble-on-beltway-politics.

Dirnbach, Eric. "Will the Future of the Working Class Be Determined by the Global South?" *Waging Nonviolence*, January 22, 2016. https://wagingnonviolence.org/feature/rise-autonomous-worker-global-south-ness.

Driver, Michael. "Reassessing the Relevance of Labor Unions." *Medium*, May 25, 2017. https://medium.com/@mdmichael-driver/reassessing-the-relevance-of-labor-unions-41ed-81ed86e9.

Galles, Gary M. "Unions Are the Worst Labor Day Deal." Foundation for Economic Education, August 31, 2017. https://fee.org/articles/unions-are-the-worst-labor-day-deal.

Goodner, David. "Resurrection Unionism—5 Ways Labor Can Rise Again." *Waging Nonviolence*, April 15, 2015. https://wagingnonviolence.org/feature/resurrection-unionism-5-ways-labor-can-rise.

Hallett, Nicole. "Future of Unions in Balance as Trump Prepares to Reshape National Labor Board." *The Conversation*, June 12, 2017. https://theconversation.com/future-of-unions-in-balance-as-trump-prepares-to-reshape-national-labor-board-78167.

"International Covenant on Economic, Social and Cultural Rights." United Nations Human Rights: Office of the High Commissioner, December 6, 1966. http://www.ohchr.org/EN/ProfessionalInterest/Pages/CESCR.aspx.

Jung, Jiwook. "Labor Unions' Decline Since the 1980s Has Given Corporate Management a Free Hand to Make Massive, Permanent Layoffs." London School of Economics US Center: USAPP, December 3, 2015. http://blogs.lse.ac.uk/usappblog/2015/12/03/labor-unions-decline-since-the-1980s-has-given-corporate-management-a-free-hand-to-make-massive-permanent-layoffs.

Lazes, Peter and Andrew Crook. "Unions Play Pivotal Role Making Companies More Competitive." *The Conversation*, April 10, 2015. https://theconversation.com/unions-play-pivotal-role-making-companies-more-competitive-39744.

Life Long Wobbly. "To Escape Trump's America, We Need to Bring the Militant Labor Tactics of 1946 Back to the Future."

Love and Rage, November 23, 2016. https://loveandragemedia.org/2016/11/23/to-escape-trumps-america-we-need-to-bring-the-militant-labor-tactics-of-1946-back-to-the-future.

Masters, Marick. "How Union Stakes in Ailing Papers Like the *Chicago Sun-Times* May Keep Them Alive." *The Conversation*, September 20, 2013. https://theconversation.com/how-union-stakes-in-ailing-papers-like-the-chicago-sun-times-may-keep-them-alive-81066.

Miller, James E. "Unions Are Not Capitalism." *Mises Canada*, September 2, 2014. https://www.mises.ca/unions-are-not-capitalism.

Morris, David. "Can a Labor Union Save the US Mail?" *On the Commons*, March 12, 2015. http://www.onthecommons.org/when-unions-are-strong-americans-enjoy-fruits-their-labor#sthash.aJgW4vVj.dpbs.

Morris, David. "When Unions Are Strong, Americans Enjoy the Fruits of Their Labor." *On the Commons*. March 31, 2011. http://www.onthecommons.org/magazine/can-a-labor-union-save-the-us-mail#sthash.ZIrHog3B.hR6poCtu.dpbs.

Reagan, Ronald. "Remarks and a Question-and-Answer Session with Reporters on the Air Traffic Controllers Strike." *Wikisource*, 1981. https://en.wikisource.org/wiki/Ronald_Reagan%27s_ultimatum_to_striking_air_traffic_controllers..

Rosenfeld, Jake. "The Rise and Fall of US Labor Unions, and Why They Still Matter." *The Conversation,* March 27, 2015. https://theconversation.com/the-rise-and-fall-of-us-labor-unions-and-why-they-still-matter-38263.

Rugh, Peter. "Low-Wage Workers, Top-Down Unions." *Waging Nonviolence*, September 30, 2013. https://wagingnonviolence.org/feature/low-wage-workers-top-unions.

Skwaire, Sarah. "Labor Unions Create Unemployment: It's a Feature, Not a Bug." Foundation for Economic Education,

June 3, 2015. https://fee.org/articles/labor-unions-create-unemployment-its-a-feature-not-a-bug.

Stid, Daniel. "Nonprofits' Stake in Controversy Surrounding Public Sector Unions." The Bridgespan Group, June 30, 2011. https://www.bridgespan.org/insights/blog/government-and-philanthropy/blog-nonprofits-39;-stake-in-controversy-surroundi.

Tilly, Chris. "It's Anti-American to Be Anti-Union." *Progressive Charleston*, September 3, 2012. http://www.progressive-charlestown.com/2012/09/labor-unions-and-american-dream.html.

US Congress. "S.545 - National Right-to-Work Act." Sponsored by Senator Paul Ryan, March 7, 2017. https://www.congress.gov/bill/115th-congress/senate-bill/545/text.

"Workers Are Never Required to Join Unions." Center for Economic and Policy Reform, April 22, 2011. http://cepr.net/blogs/beat-the-press/workers-are-never-required-to-join-unions.

Zagorsky, Jay L. "Have We Forgotten the True Meaning of Labor Day?" *The Conversation*, August 29, 2017. https://theconversation.com/have-we-forgotten-the-true-meaning-of-labor-day-64526.

Zahn, Max. "The Future of the Low-Wage Worker Movement May Depend on an Unheralded NYC Law." *Waging Nonviolence*, August 2, 2017. https://wagingnonviolence.org/feature/future-low-wage-worker-movement-nyc-law.

Zullo, Roland. "Right-to-work's Rapid Spread Is Creating More Union Free Riders." *The Conversation*, April 3, 2015. https://theconversation.com/right-to-works-rapid-spread-is-creating-more-union-free-riders-38805.

CHAPTER NOTES

INTRODUCTION

1. Schneiderman, Rose. "We Have Found You Wanting." *Remembering the 1911 Triangle Factory Fire*: Cornell University. Retrieved June 4, 2018.

CHAPTER 3: WHAT THE COURTS SAY

AMERICAN FEDERATION OF LABOR, ET AL. V. AMERICAN SASH & DOOR COMPANY ET AL. FROM THE US SUPREME COURT

CASE SYLLABUS

1 American Federation of Labor v. American Sash & Door Co., 67 Ariz. 20, 189 P.2d 912.
2 Ariz.Code Ann. § 56-120 (1939).
3 Ariz.Sess.Laws 1947, ch. 81, p. 173.

RUTLEDGE CONCURRING OPINION

1 The warrant, insofar as is material, charged that the appellants had entered into "* * * an illegal combination or conspiracy in restraint of the right to work and of trade or commerce in the State of North Carolina and against the public policy of the State of North Carolina, by executing a written agreement or contract by and between said employer and said Labor Unions and Organizations or combinations, whereby persons not members of said unions or organizations are denied the right to work for said employer, or whereby membership is made a condition of employment or continuation of said employment by said employer and whereby said named unions acquired an employment monopoly in any and all enterprises which may be undertaken by said employer are required to become or remain a member of a labor union or labor organization as a condition of employment or continuation of employment

by said employer whereby said unions acquire an employment monopoly in any and all enterprises entered into by said employer in violation of House Bill #229, Session 1947, General Assembly of North Carolina, Chapter 328, 1947 Session Laws of North Carolina, and particularly sections 2-3 & 5 thereof, and Chapter 75 of the General Statutes of N.C. * * *.'

2 See note 3.

3 The syllogism might well be: The decisions in the present cases permit a state to make 'illegal' any discrimination against nonunion workers on account of that status in relation to securing or retaining employment; strikes for 'illegal objects' are 'unlawful'; 'unlawful' strikes may be enjoined; a strike by union members against working with nonunion employees is a strike for an 'illegal object'; therefore such a strike may be enjoined.

CHAPTER 6: WHAT ORDINARY PEOPLE SAY

"IT'S ANTI-AMERICAN TO BE ANTI-UNION" BY CHRIS TILLY

(1) Freeman, Richard B. 2007. America Works: Critical Thoughts on the Exceptional U.S. Labor Market. New York: Russell Sage Foundation. Figure 5.1.

"LABOR DAY 2015" BY CAITLIN AH

1 For a quick and easy read, see this 2015 article from *Al Jazeera America*. As usual, Al Jazeera is scrupulous about citing its sources; they include this report (available here as pdf) from the City University of New York's Murphy Institute for Worker Education and Labor Studies, and this earlier article by Al-Jazeera. The National Women's Law Center also writes about unionized women and equal pay.

2 For two different takes on cost of living, see MIT's Living Wage Calculator (it looks low to me, at least from what I know of Chicago) and the Economic Policy Institute's Family Budget Calculator.

[3] For more on the Bay View Massacre, see the Wisconsin Labor History Society.

[4] For more on the Triangle Factory Fire, see *The Atlantic*'s article about Frances Perkins and Cornell University's Remembering the 1911 Triangle Factory Fire.

[5] We also learned super useful things, such as how to read contract language. I got really good at reading contract language after spending three and a half years doing it.

GLOSSARY

antitrust—Relating to laws that prevent monopolies.

compelled—To be forced to do something.

direct action—The use of strikes, demonstrations, or other public forms of protest to achieve one's demands.

displaced—Relating to the moving of a person or thing from one place to another.

dues—A payment or fee; union dues are fees that must be paid by union members to the union they are a part of.

elite—A class of people seen as having the most wealth and privilege.

franchise—Businesses that license brand names, stores, and/or business models.

general strike—A strike of workers in all or most industries.

gig economy—An economic environment where short term or contract work becomes the norm.

labor union—An organization of workers, often in a trade or profession, formed to protect and further their rights and interests.

neoliberal—Relating to a form of liberalism that favors free market capitalism

pension—A regular payment made during retirement from a fund created from the workers wages.

prejudice—Dislike or hostility based on false beliefs.

private sector—Part of the economy not under government control.

progressive—Someone favoring social reform or liberal ideas.

union busting—Relating to activities taken to prevent or disrupt the forming of labor unions.

FURTHER READING

BOOKS

Dray, Philip. *There Is Power in a Union: The Epic Story of Labor in America*. New York, NY: Anchor, 2011.

Dubofsky, Melvyn, and Joseph A. McCartin. *Labor in America: A History*. Malden, MA: Wiley-Blackwell, 2017.

Garcia, Matthew. *From the Jaws of Victory: The Triumph and Tragedy of Cesar Chavez and Farm Worker Movement*. Oakland, CA: University of California, 2014.

Geoghegan,Thomas. *The Only Thing That Can Save Us: Why America Needs a New Kind of Labor Movement*. New York, NY: New Press, 2015.

Hogler, Raymond L. *The End of American Labor Unions: The Right-to-Work Movement and the Erosion of Collective Bargaining*. Santa Barbara, CA: Praeger, 2015.

Jones, William P. *The March on Washington: Jobs, Freedom, and the Forgotten History of Civil Rights*. New York, NY: W. W. Norton, 2013.

Lichtenstein, Nelson. *State of the Union: A Century of American Labor*. Princeton, NJ: Princeton University, 2013.

McCartin, Joseph A. *Collision Course: Ronald Reagan, the Air Traffic Controllers, and the Strike That Changed America*. Oxford, UK: Oxford University Press, 2013.

Sergel, Ruth. *See You in the Streets: Art, Action, and Remembering the Triangle Shirtwaist Factory Fire*. Iowa City, IA: University of Iowa, 2016.

Uetricht, Micah. *Strike for America: Chicago Teachers Against Austerity*. Brooklyn. NY: Verso, 2014.

WEBSITES

Debt Collective
debtcollective.org
Learn more about the student debt strikes at the Debt Collective website. You can sign up to fight your own debt and read more about the organization, as well as find links to resources on different debt collectives and debt research.

Fight for $15
fightfor15.org
Learn about the nation's newest labor union at their official website. You can read more about workers' rights and sign up for their email newsletter.

INDEX

ABOUT THE EDITOR

Rita Santos has written several books for children and young adults and edited many books for adults. She earned a Masters of Science in Publishing from Pace University. When she's not writing or editing she loves traveling. Her greatest adventure so far was meeting sloths at the Sloth Sanctuary in Costa Rica. She is also a debt activist, advocating for the rights of student and medical debtors. Santos lives in New York City with her family and her cat, Aaron Purr.